The Efficient Professional Series

The Battle for Your Email Inbox

Managing Your Email Without Drowning

Robby Slaughter

Publisher
Method Press / An Imprint of AccelaWork
6100 Keystone #654
Indianapolis, IN 46220

For further information, please visit www.accelawork.com or
call 1-888-200-9387.

Cover design by AccelaWork
Photograph by Keith Tsuji Photography. Used with permission
courtesy of iStockPhoto.com.

First Printing: 2014

To Eric Marasco, who gave our
first presentation on email productivity.

Introduction: A Practical Guide

EMAIL IS LIKE WATER ON THE OPEN SEAS—it's everywhere and totally inescapable. You can pretend it doesn't exist, but ignore your email for too long and pretty soon you'll be staring at hundreds or thousands of messages. You'll be struggling just to try and read some of them. You'll never feel like you could ever be caught up.

Yet there are probably people in your professional and personal life who seem coolly efficient in managing their electronic correspondence. Their replies arrive like trains running on a schedule. They answer questions and dash off notes quickly, yet they always seem to offer complete thoughts. Best of all, they aren't constantly buried in their mobile devices. Some even leave their laptops at home when travelling on vacation.

There's also lots of advice about managing your email. The problem is that much of this advice is terrible, or impractical to apply.

What's worse is that email has become a poor surrogate for genuine communication. Instead of picking up the phone or walking a dozen feet to chat with a colleague, we express ourselves with clipped sentences and emoticons. We've leveraged some of the most advanced technology ever invented mostly to help us be more passive-aggressive.

If you've ever stared down an insurmountable inbox, you've thought to yourself: there's got a better way.

There is.

In the pages ahead, you'll find a strategy for battling your inbox that's built around a unifying principle that actually works. The chapters explain a series of tactics that, when used together, can help you keep your email system clean and make your correspondence effective. They not only include straightforward but surprising actions you can put into practice, but also ready-to-use scripts for common email conversations. Plus, you'll review what never to discuss over email, which will keep your computer drama-free and help your workplace relationships to become more powerful.

And best of all, you can find a way to achieve an almost mythical state of being.

That's right: an inbox with zero messages.

So what are you waiting for? Change your relationship with email. Change your relationship with your email partners. Take control over your electronic messaging. Do battle with your inbox—and win!

About the Series

The Efficient Professional books explain *precisely how* to increase your personal productivity at work.

There a variety of resources available which are filled with business advice. But unlike many others, The Efficient Professional lists exactly what steps you should take and provides hard evidence as to why.

Furthermore, this series focuses both on what to do as well as what *not* to do. Often, knowing what to avoid is even more important than knowing what to embrace.

Each book in the series contains a core idea that drives every recommendation. That means you don't need to memorize a vast number of rules or tips. Instead, the reader can build new habits around a single, easy-to-remember mission statement.

This way, referring back to different chapters and sections can be done quickly. Just recall the key concept, and turn to the appropriate page.

Finally, The Efficient Professional series offers fresh perspectives and does not merely rehash common sense. If you're ready to catapult your personal productivity, pick up any book in the series.

More information at **efficientprofessional.com.**

About the Author

Robby Slaughter is a workflow and productivity expert. His consulting practice assists a wide variety of organizations, including Fortune 500 companies, regional non-profits, small businesses, and individual entrepreneurs to help increase productivity, simplify workflow and optimize business processes.

Robby's particular focus is the use of stakeholder-driven business improvement through the lens of process mapping. Working with individuals and small teams, he facilitates discussions in which problems and opportunities are rapidly identified. The collaborative and visual nature of this approach has a profound impact on organizations, which frequently see dramatic and sustained productivity gains within a few weeks.

Although this consulting process does not primarily employ technology, a background in computing drives this scientific approach to improvement. After an extensive career in IT systems development, Robby realized that the principal challenges affecting individual workers are not technological in nature, but psychological. He discovered that to become more effective and efficient at work, we need to empower individuals with authority and responsibility. His consulting practice now focuses exclusively on assessing workflow challenges, helping stakeholders to design and develop new business processes, and implement systematic, people-centered changes throughout the organization.

Robby is a regular contributor to several local and national magazines and has over one hundred published articles. He has been interviewed by multiple national and international publications, including the *Wall Street Journal*. Robby is a nationally known speaker. He is also the author of several books, including *Failure: The Secret to Success*, *The Unbeatable Recipe for Networking Events*, *The How-To Guide for Generations at Work* and *The New Science of Time Management*. More information about Robby Slaughter is online at **robbyslaughter.com**.

Technical Note

The first email was sent in 1971. Now, over one hundred billion emails land in inboxes each day. The growth of email has been staggering, but the technical sophistication of email has remained largely unchanged. Modern email programs have more features, but in essence they merely ensure the reliable delivery and receipt of messages among one or more parties.

Since the fundamentals of email remain constant, this book does not make extensive reference to specific applications, websites, add-ons, services, or names of features. Readers who are capable of taking control of their inbox should also have the necessary skills to search the web for applicable solutions.

Table of Contents

PART I

WHERE EMAIL WENT WRONG

Every solution to every problem is simple.
It's the distance between the two where the mystery lies.

– Derek Landy

Chapter 1

The Problem with (Most) Email Advice

The only thing to do with good advice is to pass it on.
It is never of any use to oneself.

– Oscar Wilde

SINCE YOU'RE READING THIS BOOK, it's probably not the first time you've sought advice about how to manage your email. You've shared horror stories with colleagues about disturbingly angry messages and epic carbon-copy threads. You've clicked on countless Internet articles that promise "One Weird Email Trick that Will Change Your Life."

But none of these have made much of a dent. That's because most of the suggestions for email management claim to be a magical cure. What's worse, much of it is bad advice anyway.

It's worth reviewing some of these awful ideas to set the stage for a radically different approach. For example, consider the common proposal to sort your email into a folder hierarchy. You might have folders for each client, and then subfolder for each project.

This idea feels like the epitome of organization. But in reality, you've just significantly increased your workload. Now, you need to deal with the contents of messages (by replying, or taking some action outside of your inbox), and also thumb through an ever-growing virtual accordion file.

You've added "email librarian" to your own job description. But unlike the real professionals who curate collections that serve the general public, your own mishmash of folders has just one patron. You're polishing the dining room china in a house that's on fire.

Another popular (but boneheaded) idea is to declare "email bankruptcy." Under this scheme, simply trash all of the messages in your inbox to create a blank slate. The theory is that anything important will be resent, so you can safely delete the thousands of unprocessed messages cluttering up your email.

Furthermore, some advocates of this method suggest an email to every one of your contacts letting them know you've junked your correspondence. This plea is supposed to inspire them to resend anything pressing.

Just like the financial technique for which it is named, the principal issue with email bankruptcy is that it **fails to address the bad behaviors** which created the situation in the first place.

Furthermore, it's downright rude. You're insisting others be organized on your behalf and deduce what you need to know. Bankruptcy creates a strain on the economy of email, and lowers your credibility among your email partners.

One final example of terrible inbox management advice: never check email in the morning. Supposedly your first few hours at work should be reserved for planning your day, completing time-sensitive projects, and attending meetings. Email is not urgent, the premise implies, so it can be ignored until the afternoon.

A quick scan through the typical inbox, however, invalidates this claim. Messages sent the evening before seem to insist that the recipient provide a speedy response. News updates—whether internal or external—roll in during those crucial morning hours. Whole project plans may be reworked or scrapped entirely before lunch. Morning emails matter.

That's not to say you should respond to email continuously throughout the day. Nor does it mean you should read email every fifteen minutes. But, it will take time to retrain other people not to use email as if it was instant messaging. Simply ignoring your inbox until the clock strikes noon is foolish.

There are two issues with these quick fixes. First, like all magic tricks, they aren't applicable in the real world. A performer is able to amaze you by finding your card because he has stacked the deck in advance. Your actual inbox isn't a perfect set piece that was laid out by a stagehand.

Second, most ready-to-use email management advice doesn't address genuine problems with the email experience. The problem isn't that we lack a coherent folder structure; **the problem is that we think of email as a form of digital recordkeeping.**

The issue is not that our inboxes are hopelessly large, it's that we incorrectly visualize every individual message as an equal-sized portion of an embarrassingly large debt. And finally, it's not that incoming messages that inescapably ruin an otherwise productive morning—it's that we don't invest the time required to change the culture.

To address the first weakness of half-baked solutions to the email crisis, we need a brand new perspective on electronic mail. But more on that in a minute. To deal with the second weakness, we have to look at real problems.

Some of these are head-scratchers, others are hair-pullers, but quite a few are top-of-the-lungs-screamers. Consider the person who sends an email, and ten minutes later sends an "I forgot to also say" follow-up.

Then there is the message with a 200-page attachment which closes with "Thoughts?" Also: reply-all chains that stretch into a dozen "RE: RE: RE: RE:" prefixes, passive-aggressive one sentence messages, blank subject lines, old conversation threads re-used for completely new topics, and more.

What's the answer? **The way to win the battle with your inbox is not tricks, but a strategy.** It is more than a couple of techniques, it's a wholesale change in your point of view. And the foundation of your new way of thinking about email is to consider everything from your inbox to your Sent Items folder to the *bcc:* line to the other people in your network as parts of an email system.

Your goal is to understand how the machine works, where it struggles, what parts need oil, and what must be replaced altogether. You are not merely the driver of the vehicle that is your email program. You are also the mechanic. You must become an inbox engineer.

Systems, of course, are central to nearly every successful human endeavor. Governments are formed through a system of laws, policies debated through a system of parliamentary procedure. Businesses design and execute business rules in the form of operations manuals and corporate policies. Chefs use recipes, athletes run plays, and soldiers follow orders. Even musicians agree to common tunings and standard notation. Successful ongoing operations depend on systems.

Every system is composed of two interlocking elements: **parts** and **processes.** A part is a component, meaning that it is either part of something larger, contains smaller parts, or both. A process is a behavior. It's often described as a rule or a pattern.

As a system: the parts of email are elements such as messages, recipients, subject lines, folders, attachments, so on. The processes include replying, forwarding, deleting, moving.

Yet many of us do not treat our email like a system. We grab the mouse and begin clicking furiously. And by failing to think like a mechanic, our inbox steadily falls into disrepair. Our email is soon cursed by the same problem that wrecks so many large operations: too much inconsistency.

There are plenty of parts of life where we want to be surprised, but not within the confines of a well-running system. A consistent system is **predictable**: you can use it to tell the future. A consistent system is **resilient**: it does not collapse when subjected to bad information. And, a consistent system is **inflexible**: it does not immediately yield to those who don't follow its rules.

This last quality might sound troubling. Don't we *want* flexibility—especially when we communicate with others? The problem is in the definition. The word "flexible" means "bends but does not break." This is a property of bad systems. Consider those parents who tell their kids there will be consequences but never dole out punishment, or government officials who ignore the rules for personal friends.

A flexible system for email is one where we are constantly making exceptions for other people. We allow them to walk all over us, whether they intend to or not. We scramble to meet unreasonable expectations. The choice to be inflexible is a radical departure for most people, but one that is absolutely necessary given the scourge that is email.

This advice, by the way, should not be applied elsewhere. You should still accommodate house guests, comply with other's dietary restrictions, and make pleasant conversation with strangers.

That's what makes a good system. Predictability, resiliency, and a certain degree of inflexibility. It's what you need for most any large enterprise, and what you need when tackling your own electronic messages.

Systems are everywhere. Treating email like a system (instead of a sort of virtual quicksand) will radically change your experience.

So how do you turn your email into a system?

By identifying parts and processes. By breaking down email into its constituent components and determining the processes and steps needed.

The first step? You're ready to take it.

Turn the page.

Chapter 2

A Mantra for Email Management

Your philosophy determines whether you will
go for the disciplines or continue the errors.

– Jim Rohn

THE ROOT WORDS THAT MAKE UP "EMAIL"—electronic mail—are no accident. The mailbox outside your home is not a long-term storage facility. It's more like the glass that holds your beer. It's a transitory object, and most of the time, should be empty.

If you ever had a penpal in the days before email dominated your written correspondence, you remembered how it took days for questions and answers to make the round trip. You thought carefully about what you wrote. You waited expectantly for a letter to arrive.

Email is based on the same idea: taking time to write a message. And though you might have saved old letters for sentimental reasons, you didn't run to your box of letters every time you wanted to look up the address of a friend. Instead, you had an address book. If you received an invite to a party, you didn't keep checking the postcard where it was mentioned. You wrote it in your calendar. If a family member sent an important document, you didn't leave it in the mailbox. You filed it away for safekeeping.

These routines make up part of your system for postal mail. But even if you aren't the kind of person who owns a color-coded wall calendar and a multi-slot mail sorter, you can still get by with keeping your letters, catalogs, and junkmail in a pile. That's because there's just not that much of it. When it comes to email, however, you can't survive by the seat of your pants. You need a plan for managing your inbox.

Effective systems aren't easy to describe in detail, but their spirit can often be captured in a few words. This is a motto, or a mission or vision statement. Sometimes it's attached to the company behind the scenes rather than the project itself.

Consider the Apollo space program, as proclaimed by President Kennedy: "Before this decade is out, to land a man on the moon and return him safely to earth." In just one sentence, he explains the principles of the system. These include *what* will be done, *when* we'll complete it, and *how we know* we've succeeded.

Another example arises from a saying popularized by Bob Vila, television host of the award-winning program *This Old House*. To explain his philosophy on remodeling and woodworking, he often said, "Measure twice, cut once." These four words communicate volumes about his handiwork. The system describes a *sequence* of activities, *prioritizes* confirmation, but still demands *action*.

One of the world's largest logistics networks is associated with the following statement: "Neither snow nor rain nor heat nor gloom of night stays these couriers from the swift completion of appointed their rounds." Although the archaic language may take a some work to decipher, The United States Postal Service creed identifies *objections* (like foul weather), characterizes *what* will be done ("couriering"), *how* it will be done ("swiftly"), and even describes a *plan* ("appointed rounds."). The mantra summarizes the entire operation.

Here is a vision statement for your inbox. Write it down. Commit it to memory. Transcribe it onto a sticky note and affix it to your screen.

> Email is for routing ideas, not for creating or storing information.

That's a vision statement which is intended to change your point of view. It tells you the *purpose of email* as well as its *common abuses*. But the mantra also explains the *parts* and *processes* of email. The parts aren't just information; the key process is not creation or storage. It's about ideas and routing.

So what's an idea?

An idea is information upon which you can act. For example, "Next Tuesday at 11AM" is just a piece of information. But "Lunch at the Main Street Diner with Frank, Next Tuesday at 11AM" is an idea. If you want to make the appointment, you need to act upon it. You need to put it in your calendar. You may want to prepare for the meeting by putting together an agenda.

There are tons of ideas that come through email. Sometimes it's just a piece of data, like an address or a file (that you know what you need to do with). Other times, an idea is a question—maybe even one that is too big or complicated for a window in a computer screen.

The reason to make a distinction that *email is for ideas* is so that we **do something** with the information that comes to us through email, and also so that we **direct others** with what to do with what we send them. Email is for ideas, not just random, context-free snippets of data. If it's worth sending in an email then it must be significant.

> **Sidebar:** This is one of the reasons that spam is so annoying. We expect email messages to contain something useful, but our inbox is overwhelmed with junk. And worst of all, we sometimes generate this crap. When we forward jokes and funny images to others, we aren't passing along an idea which they can use productively. Instead, we're hoping those recipients have the same sense of humor and want us to interrupt their workflow with something that amused us. There are lots of great places for humor where it's expected—but given the panic-inducing insanity that is email, the inbox probably isn't one of them.

What's the difference between an idea and information? Information is just data. You may need data later on, but it's useless without context.

You may remember a science teacher asking this question: "If you have five gallons of water and you pour out three gallons of water, what do you have left?"

The answer is not "two." The answer is "two *gallons.*" Without the unit of measure, the number alone is meaningless. Likewise, if stuffed alongside countless other messages in your inbox or your email folders, a crucial word, phrase, or number is equally useless. You must figure out where to put data, in the same way that you must attach the word "gallons" to the number "two" in order to have a viable answer.

As the age of technology advances, we live in a world dominated by the buzzword "big data." That's a term that refers to the incredible volumes of information collected on everything from retail activities to cellphone movements to Twitter trends. And while big data may be crucial in solving crimes, fighting disease, or improving marketing, your inbox should not be an example of big data. Your inbox should be mostly something which is empty. Your inbox is a router for ideas.

What's routing?

Routing is the notion of sending something to the right place, rather than hanging on to it indefinitely. The way most people use email today is the antithesis of routing. They get an email and leave it in their inbox for weeks, or perhaps forever. Or what only *appears* to be better: they stick it in a folder and never look at it again.

Routing means you send stuff to where it belongs, usually outside of the system in question. A router in a computer network is the nerve center of the operation, but its job is to get data to the right user *outside* the network.

Routing at a delivery company is about getting freight out the door, not leaving it to rot in an ever-expanding warehouse. Routing is what a great receptionist does: transferring calls instead of parking them, delivering messages instead of losing them, serving walk-ins instead of ignoring them. Routing is about solving problems and moving on.

For inspiration, consider the most effective routing systems in the world: intake procedures in life-saving hospital emergency rooms, the millions fed daily in fast food restaurants, and checkout lines deftly managed by retail giants. Whether you like their products or align with their policies, it's hard not to be impressed with the profound throughput of these institutions. They know something about routing. They offer lessons you can put to use in front of your screen.

In your local ER, a team of highly-trained professionals makes a crucial decision as each patient comes through their doors. By following a rigorous but fast procedure, they determine if the individual in question needs triage or further diagnostics. Are they bleeding out or gasping for air? Can the medical experts find open wounds or evidence of internal trauma? Does a neurological protocol indicate damage to the brain?

These are the kinds of questions that enable doctors, nurses, and emergency personnel to decide whether to rush you into an operating room or set you aside for further analysis. That's a detailed, medically-validated process designed to make consistently good decisions in minutes. And it contains great lessons for managing your own email inbox, as good routing requires **acknowledging incoming opportunities as they arrive**, but sometimes altering the order to deal with the challenges that are most critical.

A visit to the drive-through window of your favorite restaurant tells a different story. Here, personnel aren't saving lives, but feeding the multitudes. Almost without exception, customers are served in the order they arrive.

But if you look into the back of the restaurant, you can witness smart routing in action. Components of every possible meal are staged and ready to be assembled. Food items are organized in trays, racks, and coolers. Often, entrees are already waiting under a heat lamp. In this highly efficient operation, they make it (or at least part of it) *before* you order it.

This concept isn't limited to fast food. Even in an upscale restaurant, much of the soups, breads, dressings, condiments, and beverages you consume are prepared long before you arrive. You can apply the same logic to managing your email. Commonly-used scripts can be pre-written. Messages you'll need in the future can be composed today and saved as drafts. Just as there's no need to wait until you'll feeling hungry to make a dinner reservation, there's no need to wait until messages arrive to plan your responses.

If you prefer to make your meals at home, you likely patronize a supermarket to fill your pantry. Here, brilliant routing systems appear when it's time to tally your purchases and pay your bill. Many of us witnessed the transition from manual addition to barcode scanning. But the latest innovation in retail is the self-service checkout line. Instead of a team member reviewing each item by hand, *you* are temporarily employed by the store as both cashier and bagger. The business has turned the customer into an essential piece of the system.

Retail stores make this clever investment to reduce costs. Likewise, you can flip responsibility for managing parts of your email back on the person who sent the message in the first place. Share the workload by asking questions instead of only giving answers. Direct them to resources rather than providing complete solutions. Put some of the work—and some of the control—into the hands of the individual who is seeking the value. Get them involved in being part of the router for your inbox, whether they realize it or not.

A great system is more than levers and gears. It's more than grease and maintenance. It's more than operating manuals and well-trained technicians. Amazing systems carry with them an inspiring phrase that outlines their structure and their purpose. Here's yours for your inbox:

> Email is for routing ideas, not for creating or storing information.

But a mantra is only as good as its application. If your philosophy for life is to accept others as they are, you can't spend your days judging their choices. The vision statement for email must be similarly applied in order to find success.

To transform your inbox into a well-oiled machine, you must stop using it as a scratchpad for idle thoughts. You must quit holding on to old messages in the hope that you'll need them some day.

Instead, you must begin routing ideas to the appropriate place—which is well beyond your email system.

And that's the best place to begin. To tackle the beast that is your inbox, look elsewhere.

The problems that manifest within your electronic folders arise from deeper challenges you face in managing information.

The solution starts well beyond email itself.

PART II

DEEPER CHALLENGES

I suppose it is tempting, if the only tool you have is a
hammer, to treat everything as if it were a nail.

– Abraham Maslow

Chapter 3

To Better Manage Your Email, Start Elsewhere

When solving problems, dig at the roots
instead of just hacking at the leaves.

– Anthony J. D'Angelo

THE CRISIS OF EMAIL MAY BE MOST OBVIOUS when staring at countless messages in your inbox. But the cause of our issues has very little to do with email itself. We are, largely speaking, not particularly organized. And more importantly, we're overwhelmed with material to manage, making the goal of an orderly life a total impossibility.

As a professional, you're responsible for a seemingly infinite variety of minutiae about your personal and professional life. You need to keep track of everything from paying your bills and managing your finances to keeping track of your kids' soccer schedules. You're actively assigned to dozens of projects and teams at work, racing to complete daily tasks, struggling to comply with special requests, and miles from the original job description under which you were hired.

If anything is accurate, it is the ominous phrase "Other duties as assigned."

To get your email inbox in order, you might just want to start with how you manage the rest of the ideas in your life. You'll benefit most if you first manage what you know, then what projects you must complete, the contacts within your circles, the tasks related to each project and person, the calendars that dictate your future, and the relationships with the people who matter most.

Consider the words "knowledge management." That's a big phrase that has become a whole industry in itself. There are lots of pieces of useful data that flow through your life, such as people's birthdays, book recommendations, the phone number for your pharmacy, or special instructions for the new software package at the office.

Before you can win the battle with your inbox, you should develop a system for managing your own knowledge. You must find a way to keep track of the countless little bits of information that appear, deciding what to discard, what to retain, and where to keep it.

It might seem like this has nothing to do with email. And while it's true that organizing the details of your life is a problem that long predates modern computer technology, it's now one that is closely integrated with your inbox. That's not only because your email is the *source* of much of this data—it's also because email applications now contain places to keep much of it.

Many of these programs come with integrated calendars, contact directories, task management tools, and even digital sticky notes. When a message lands in your inbox, you might immediately be typing it into another system nearby.

Therefore, when you stumble across a nugget of knowledge about your world, don't just leave it in the medium where you found it. Instead, start by asking questions. These should inspire you to do something with that data, whether you find a place to store it. Better yet, the answers may help you decide how to act and put the knowledge to work.

1. **How can I make this not just information, but an idea?**

That means taking the raw data and associating it with a useful action. If you spot a takeout menu hanging from the handle to your front door, picture yourself ordering dinner on a rainy evening. If you see a return address on an invite to a housewarming party, imagine one day sending that family a holiday greeting card.

When information is elevated to a scenario, it becomes more obvious what to do with it. The takeout menu is mostly useless at work and frustrating if left kicking around your bedroom. It should go into a dedicated space in the kitchen or your car's glove compartment. Or you should take a photo with your mobile phone and keep it in an album.

2. Is this item part of a larger category of similar items?

Matching elements to groupings is fundamental to organizing. Plates go into a cabinet, silverware goes into a drawer; both are kept in the kitchen. Information has a natural hierarchy when applied to your life. When you encounter a fact or a suggestion, attempt to classify it.

The most obvious pigeonholes are those implied by existing tools—but more on that in a moment. For now, consider whether the data applies mostly to your personal world or professional world? Is it associated with solely your own interests, or those of your team, your friends, or your family?

Can you attach it to an existing project, or does it fall in the "maybe someday" pile? Think structure and order. Consider the levels of priority and authority.

Attempt to hang each ornament at the right branch on the tree of your life.

3. What system or service should I use to store this idea?

Information may arrive in email, but it's destined for other systems. If it's a detail about a *person*, attach it to your virtual or physical address book. If it's a detail about an *event*, add it your calendar. If it's an *assignment*, put it on your to-do list. Translate raw information into actionable ideas, and transfer them into the appropriate platform.

There are many more tools available for storing new ideas. Book recommendations might go into your Amazon Wish List (or your own equivalent scratch pad). Articles to read might immediately be sent to the printer, and tossed into a folder in your briefcase marked "for the train ride home." Key reminders could be transcribed onto the whiteboard in your office. Find a system, and send information there. Then, delete it from your inbox.

4. Who else needs to know besides me?

Perhaps the gravest sin of email is that obsessive need to tell everyone through abuse of the address lines. It's just as easy to send an email to one person as it is to a hundred, and the ready availability of reply-all ensures that discussions can continue to fill up inboxes indefinitely.

When you receive some new information, part of your responsibility is deciding who else needs to know that data. This is not "who might benefit" from learning these details, but whose responsibilities are more difficult to meet if they are kept in the dark.

The temptation is to use the built-in features of email to share this data—by replying, forwarding, or composing messages. But instead, consider alternate mediums to distributing information.

For example: perhaps a reminder to keep the fridge clean would be best served as a sign in on that appliance in the break room, since this idea is only relevant to people who go there. Maybe project updates should be saved in a shared drive or on the company Intranet so that people who need them can find them. Figure out who needs to know and where they will be. Then, share information appropriately.

5. How will I access this idea in the future?

About four thousand years ago, humanity invented what may be the most transformative technology in all of history: written language. There's too much information to remember, so we have the ability to save it by jotting it down or typing it up.

That's why for every piece of data you receive you should consciously determine whether it must be at the top of your mind, accessible with some deep thought, or reachable through some kind of indexing system.

You have to develop your own method for managing your knowledge, whether via binders, folders, filing cabinets, or electronic storage. However, your mechanism should be as public and transparent as possible to those who also need that knowledge. Even though you may not need labels, you should add them for the benefit of people who aren't you.

Save data where *others* can find it. If you must save emails, do so in public folders rather than private ones; put client details into the customer relationship management (CRM) database rather than your own contacts directory.

The purpose in answering and asking these questions is to teach yourself that email is not a destination, but an origin. Your inbox is not a pile of electronic clutter, but more like time spent in the batting cages. You're practicing rapidly identifying what's being pitched at you, making contact with the ball, and sending it in the direction you choose. Email is about teaching yourself to be organized and efficient, so that you can demonstrate these qualities in the *real* work of managing your daily activity.

Your inbox is a training ground. Consider this: all of us are engaged in projects at work or at home. Each is either a one-time activity, or something which is started, conducted, and completed on a recurring basis. Some projects spawn from new ideas. Others arise as a continuation of an earlier effort.

When you receive data about a project via the window on your computer screen, your task is to separate out key details and sprinkle each ingredient into their respective locations. Deadlines, problems, documentation, and open questions each require a different kind of action. Some of the correspondence about projects represents work for you. Some indicates tasks for other people.

Evaluate, assign, and follow up. And keep the records in an organized place *outside* of your email system.

Your inbox is also where you connect with the majority of the people in your life. When you receive a message from someone new, they often litter you inadvertently with details that may eventually be crucial. Email signatures often contain physical addresses, professional titles, and even cellphone numbers. Sometimes, they have a photograph that triggers your memory or establishes a face for someone you've never met in person. A quick scan through a message can reveal virtual buried treasure.

When you find a gem hidden in an email, choose to act. Saving this data when you receive it may someday save your bacon. Plus, consider typing a few notes about how you first connected, the name of their spouse, their kids, or their hometown. You'll never know when the personal touch may have a profound impact on your life.

Messages sent to you via electronic mail may seem like a to-do list. But in reality, emails are a precursor to your own task list. Each item that lands in your inbox represents work. However, you decide how to prioritize that activity—and even if you'll do it at all. Even if you work for the world's most obsessive micromanager, you still have choices. Your to-dos are your own prerogative.

Think of it this way: your email is a private space to practice managing the incredible variety of requests that come your way. If you develop a pattern for identifying, assessing, delegating, and scheduling tasks that land in your inbox, imagine what you'll do in meetings with your boss or in collaboration with your team. If you want to get organized with respect to dealing with all of the countless duties weighing you down, there's no better trial by fire than taming the swarm of email messages.

Finally, one of the best weapons in dealing with your workload is leveraging the future. Although tomorrow is often the worst time to do something that should be done today, there is plenty of room in the weeks, months, and years ahead to tackle projects that are *not urgent* right now. Consider the multitudes of email invitations to special events. If you build a pattern to accept or decline them upon receipt and immediately add them to your calendar, you can confidently ignore all of the follow-up reminders. You know that parts of your future are planned and don't need automated nagging to make sure you keep an appointment.

Likewise, using email replies to promise to do work is an amazing technique for strengthening your organizing muscles. If you announce your own deadlines and assure others that you will meet them, you need to have a system for keeping your word. Your calendar makes this possible. Get the conversation out of email and into a plan for real action.

Email may be drowning you right now. But consider it not as an unstoppable flood of water but instead as a commercial plumbing system. Water goes in, flows through pipes, is directed through valves, utilized in applications, and drained away. We only notice the plumbing when it's sprung a leak. If you've got hundreds or thousands of messages in your inbox, you're leaking everywhere.

Just like cleaning up a mess with your pipes, the best place to start is not in the two feet of standing water. Take control of the mains, identify the valves, and determine what's causing the problem. Then, when you go to mop up you won't find yourself bailing out while water is still pouring in.

And while tackling your email by starting with your other organizational needs might seem overwhelming, the truth is that you've already made progress. If there are piles of papers on your desk, they probably correspond roughly to major projects. If you have a desk drawer full of the business cards of your contacts, that means you've been making an effort to put them in the same place. You've determined handy reference items and stuck them to your bulletin board. There are the beginnings of good systems in place.

What's next is to take these tools and refine them so they become destinations for ideas. They must have a structure that feels comfortable and productive. And you need a process for taking new information that lands in your inbox and translating it to the place where it should reside.

To do this, you need patterns. You need procedures. You need rules.

The problem is that most of the rules for handling email have already been established, mostly by accident. That's why they need to go. You're going to reinvent the way email is treated.

To change your world, turn the page.

Chapter 4

Changing the Rules

Everyone thinks of changing the world,
but no one thinks of changing himself.

– Leo Tolstoy

THERE'S AN UNWRITTEN RULE OF EMAIL: when you get a message, deal with it. That might have worked when mail was what showed up at the box outside your house. It only came once a day (but never on Sundays). If there were bills, you paid them. If there were coupons, you clipped them.

Email, however, arrives incessantly. It's like wave after wave crashing on the beach, only less predictable. It doesn't just arrive six times a day; it can come in every minute of the day, twenty four hours a day, 365 days a year. Email is overwhelming.

And that is the key problem: while we're working on one message, a new email pops up. We can't help but take a peek at it. Pretty soon we're reading and replying to the second email, only to be followed by the third email.

This is a recipe for frustration. And it's one you've likely been following without realizing it.

1. The world is unfair.

Here are two acronyms every business professional should learn: LIFO and FIFO. Respectively they stand for "last in, first out" and "first in, first out." These are terms that relate to countless industries from logistics to healthcare to computer science. They describe two common ways to process a queue.

Consider a recent trip on a passenger bus. The first people in the door tend to take the seats up front, so they are the first out. That's a FIFO system. The same is true at the checkout lane at your local grocery store: The first person in line is the first person to finish.

But if you're moving across country by loading your stuff into an enormous rental truck, the first piece of furniture you load goes right to the back. That means it's the *last* one to be unloaded.

The same is true for most movie fans. Arrive early enough and you get the prime seat in the very middle of the center aisle. But that also means you can't leave the theater until *after* everyone who arrived later than you did. The last one in is the first one out: LIFO.

This overview of one essential element of the field of queueing theory is applicable to many aspects of your personal and professional life. But when it comes to your inbox, should you be running a LIFO or a FIFO operation?

If you follow the default of most email programs, you'll notice that the most recent messages appear at the top of your inbox. That automatically encourages the user to deal with the last—or most recent message—as the first. That's a LIFO system.

But LIFO systems tend to be frustrating. You make the effort to arrive early to the box office and score a great seat, which means you not only have to wait longer for the show to start—but you're stuck waiting the longest *after* the program. You only get to leave once everyone else who *didn't* show up as early as you did is on their way home.

This is the same reason it's so annoying to see someone cut ahead of you in a queue. It's why we hate it when the employee at the customer service desk answers a ringing phone instead of helping the next person in line. LIFO often seems unfair.

In most cases, FIFO is the way to go. The same is true for your email: the *oldest* email in your inbox was the first one to arrive. Therefore, it should be the *first* message you process. Reverse your inbox order to put old emails at the top. Deal with your emails one at a time, working on progressively more recent emails as you go along.

This change may sound simple, but the experience can be profound. Instead of panicking at those emails which claim to be urgent but only arrived an hour ago, you can work through messages which are *genuinely urgent* because you've managed to miss dealing with them for days, weeks, or longer.

Switching from LIFO to FIFO also changes the way other people treat you as an email partner, although this happens more slowly. Whether they realize it consciously or not, people who send you messages will start to expect a response *later* rather than *sooner*. If you stick with the default LIFO approach and tackle the most recent message as you can, your response times will be inconsistent and therefore frustrating to others.

Dumping LIFO in favor of FIFO is worthy of consideration outside the inbox. But changing this rule will change your experience using email.

2. Making email like regular mail.

The US Postal Service may seem like an antiquated reference in a book about email, but there's plenty to learn from the organization that delivers over 500 million letters and packages every day. One of the most profound lessons? Frequency of delivery. No matter how many times you head down to the mailbox, new mail will only arrive at most once a day.

For your local post office, this is mostly a matter of resources. To stop at your home or business multiple times per day would require some combination of more letter carriers, smaller routes, and higher fees.

But the electronic mailmen have no such limitations, since the infrastructure of the Internet grows at an exponential rate. Email can arrive constantly, and the incessant ding reminding you that "you've got mail" can drive you mad.

Of course it's sometimes convenient to be able to send a block of text or a file attachment halfway around the world in seconds, but most of the time you don't actually *need* emails to be delivered instantly. If you absolutely must have a conversation with someone else at this very instant, a much better technology is the telephone. It's far more efficient than a barrage of back-and-forth messages, plus you can hear the inflection in the other person's voice.

If email were like traditional mail, it wouldn't be quite so overwhelming. You might still receive dozens or hundreds of messages per day in total, but they'd all come at once instead of in a torturous endless hailstorm.

It turns out that you *can* make email like traditional mail, sort of. Most modern email systems have a "work offline" mode. This was originally invented for those times that you'd be disconnected, such as a long airplane flight or train ride. Although wireless internet is now seemingly available everywhere, setting your email program to "work offline" can have a tremendous impact on your productivity.

Here's how it works: while your system is in the special "offline" mode, messages that are destined for your inbox wait patiently at your electronic post office. You can reply to the emails you already have, process them, file them, or delete them as you prefer. You can even send your own emails—although just like with your postal mailbox, they won't be "picked up" until later.

Go back "online" and all of your outgoing mail and incoming mail will be delivered. But in the meantime, you will have swept everything clean and gotten a handle on what you have to do.

Working in the "offline mode" seems contrary to the latest developments in technology. Today you can connect to the Internet at breakneck speeds practically anywhere on the planet. Sometimes, your laptop or smartphone may pick up signals without you actively changing your settings, giving you instant, unexpected access to whatever information you desire.

Yet, there is a considerable advantage to unplugging for brief periods of time. Just like the artist who goes to a cabin to finish a masterpiece, or the jury that heads to a secluded room to deliberate in private, you too should consider disengaging from the constant distractions of incoming mail in order to process the email that you *already* have.

Changing the rule from "always connected" to "only connected when I need to be" also helps to change your email experience. Now it's more like working a familiar problem or churning through a project. And like changing the order to FIFO (first in, first out), your response times will begin to change. Instead of answering right away, your messages will go out in chunks at the end of each of your offline sessions. You control when you receive mail, and when you send it.

Rewriting the rule about how messages are grouped puts you in control. It communicates to others that you are busy doing work, and don't have the availability to treat their incoming messages like a game of whack-a-mole. But if you respond consistently and maintain a professional attitude, you're not marginalizing people either. You're making a clear distinction that email is for non-urgent, important correspondence. If they need you right now, they know how to find you.

3. Processing via search.

No feature of modern email systems is more powerful (and therefore more dangerous) than the ability to search your messages. Consider Google. The company that made their name and their fortune on a wildly successful search engine for the entire web have brought the same incredible data-seeking technology to your inbox. Other email systems offer similar features, and now you can search through tens of thousands of old messages in a fraction of a second.

There's a significant difference between searching the web for information and searching your own email archive: you don't actually know if what you want exists out there on the Internet. If you're searching your own email, you're trying to find something you know you have but can't put your hands on any other way.

In this regard, using search to find old emails is a crutch that enables the user to not be organized about managing the information in their own life. It's as if everything you ever jotted down is on a million sticky notes laying randomly around a dusty attic. That's not a system. That is chaos.

The fact that modern computers allow you to instantly locate any of these virtual sticky notes if you happen to remember *an exact word or phrase on them* isn't a sign that your days of having to be organized are coming to a close. Instead, this shows how disorganized most people are. If you *don't need* to use the search function of your email to find everything, you're *more* organized—and therefore will be more productive—than almost everyone you know.

So if search shouldn't be used as part of everyday email management, what is its role? There are only two good reasons to use search: processing a stale email system and the occasional need for proof.

If your email has managed to collect hundreds or thousands of messages, the search feature can be a fantastic way to clear out whole swaths of useless messages in seconds. For example, consider those promotional offers you receive from your favorite department store, restaurant, or online merchant. These probably arrive like clockwork on a weekly or monthly basis, with additional messages for holidays and special events. Search for the company name and you can delete all of their emails at once.

A similar technique works well for those long email chains, where have been copied on a discussion that has gone back and forth for dozens of messages. First, make sure that the *oldest* messages are at the top of your inbox. Then search for a phrase that appears in the subject line— the one preceded by "Re: Re: Re: Re: …" It may help to put the phrase in quotes to get an exact match.

Then, you can safely delete all but the last (or most recent) message in the exchange. That's because the back and forth will be completely contained in the body of the message. You can review the discussion it by scrolling to the end and reading from the bottom up.

There is one more use of search that you should consider, but it can be hazardous to your career. That's an automated scan of your Sent Items to *prove* what you or someone else said.

Email serves as a written record of your past actions as well as those of others. If you ever get caught in a situation where you need to show what was actually agreed in writing, your Sent Items folder probably contains the evidence.

However, consider this a nuclear option. No one appreciates having their own words thrown back in their face. Keep your Sent Items forever in case of emergency, but hope you never have to search through them to settle a dispute.

For the most part, you don't need search if you almost never have to go digging through piles of old messages. Work to forget this feature exists. Search no more.

4. Working from "sent."

The Sent Items folder is the most useful part of your entire email infrastructure. The inbox represents work that others have assigned to you, whether they need you to review documents, provide feedback, set up meetings, or just decide if you want to purchase whatever product is on special. But your Sent Items folder represents what you are waiting on *others* to do. It's a record of what the future holds.

Since you're reading this book, you know that email is both a wonderful tool and a terrible curse. One of the significant challenges for many professionals is maintaining accountability. It will take you about a month into your first grown-up job to realize that lots of people simply don't do what they say they are going to do.

When you send someone an email, however, you're establishing a request or a promise that is typically more firm than one merely said aloud. The effort it takes to type up your intentions—or restate the promises that someone else made—is enough effort to make it real. Once an email message is received, it's at least a little hard to ignore.

Your Sent Items folder is effectively a follow-up list and a to-do list rolled into one. It consists of promises you've made to others and work you are waiting on them to complete. The rest of your messages serve to close the loop on some bit of work you've just wrapped up.

Depending on how your email system is organized, you may want to use flags, colors, or stars to mark those sent messages requiring further action. Or, if you're really focused on execution, create a subfolder underneath your Sent Items just to hold those messages where you are anticipating a reply. That way, you can check this folder periodically in case you need to remind other people to take action.

Working from this mailbox instead of your inbox also implies something else: that your actual inbox isn't that urgent. In fact, it may often be *empty*. Your Sent Items will always contain a journal of your activity. Changing the rule that you "must live in your inbox" will change your perspective. You'll focus on the future you're creating rather than the past expectations of others.

These are the unwritten rules of email. But like many customs, they don't stand up to scrutiny. A little analysis shows that the way we've always done it may be a terrible way to operate.

What's particularly amazing about deciding not to follow the rules is that in addition to changing your own experience, you begin to influence others. After all, if they see you pushing the envelope and breaking with tradition, they may consider doing the same.

And that's much of the point of changing email patterns. After all, electronic messaging is the oldest form of online social media. It's an experience we create together. Modifying your own behavior can inspire others to do the same.

And if you can get *other* people to act smarter, imagine the possibilities.

Chapter 5

Inspiring Behavior, Establishing Boundaries

Most bad behavior comes from insecurity.

– Debra Winger

COUNTLESS PEOPLE WHO ARE IN TROUBLED RELATIONSHIPS decide not to seek counseling, because they feel that no matter what they do, they cannot change the behavior of other people.

This may be how you feel about your relationships with your colleagues, business partners, vendors, and customers. They may be demanding, disorganized, or annoying. Their actions might make you feel guilty or make you feel sorry for them. And unfortunately, we're stuck with this. We cannot change the behavior of others.

While this is technically true, a good therapist will explain that although you're not responsible for other people's actions, you do have the power to influence them. Two of the most effective ways for doing so are through intentional inspiration and clear boundaries.

To understand how to help transform the behavior of other people through email, let's start with everyday office communication. After all, the people you are emailing with are real people who you would otherwise converse with in person, over the phone, or through some other communication medium.

It's worth noting the incredibly poor state of professional communication. You've experienced this on conference calls, in the break room, and of course over email. Consider the following:

People ask questions they don't want answered honestly, such as "how are you doing?" or "did you have a good weekend?"

People give answers designed to end conversation, rather than facilitate understanding. "Oh, I'm fine." "I'm really busy!" "Just working!"

People interrupt conversations instead of waiting for their turn. Next time you're listening to two people talking at work, try paying close attention to this phenomenon. You'll notice that rarely does someone get a chance to complete their thought before they are overrun completely by another person shoving into the space.

People spread rumors and gossip. Although we all learned that you should never say something about someone that you wouldn't say to their face, professionals often speak poorly of others.

People fill the space by talking without saying much. They gab about nothing in particular, taking up time that you could be using to get something done.

Behaving strangely in person is bad enough. When you behave strangely in email, you create a permanent record of your mood at that moment. If you're upset, your words will feel angry. If you're annoyed, you will be curt or obsess over details. If you are excited you'll pepper your messages with exclamation points. Conversation may disappear into the air, but email is forever.

> **Sidebar:** This is not to disparage the craft of writing, which can be used to teleport complex ideas and deep emotional weight across vast distances and entire generations. While email consists of the same letters, words, and sentences that make up great novels and riveting journalism, we don't think of email the same way. Email is both intimate and impersonal. We write and read it from every corner of our lives, yet it's too easy to vomit our emotions onto the keyboard. You can use writing to share great ideas and powerful feelings, but don't try to do it over email.

The culture of interpersonal communication at the office has its own series of strategies. Everyone knows who to avoid in the break room, and who is likely to "drop by" our cubicle for a chat. Most people can identify the office gossip and the colleague who you need to befriend in order to ensure the next promotion. Who talks and how they speak is the politics of business.

For people who don't feel they have either the stomach or the brainpower to navigate this part of their career, email can be a wonderful respite. Instead of having to answer questions on the spot, the inbox provides the precious benefit of *time* to reply. Instead of being required to craft witty comments that include everyone in the room, email is a place of plain communication and replies directed to specific individuals. Email can be a place to help turn the tide on the many small injustices of office life.

The way you treat email informs other people, albeit indirectly. If you respond promptly, they expect you to *always* respond promptly. If you can be relied on to do favors over email that would be hard to ask for in person, they will start to ask you for those favors over email. Others will adjust their behaviors based on yours, which means if you control your own behaviors, you can often influence the behaviors of others.

There are two critical dynamics over which you have power: **when** you send email, and **what** you write. Most everything else is dictated by the situation. But your choices with regard to timing and content can change the way others treat you. After all, you're teaching them how to behave by when you write.

The question of sending email at a particular time may be one that you've never considered before. But think about those messages that arrive on weekends or are time-stamped as 2:00am. They reveal something about the workload and the sleep habits of the sender.

Emails that land in your inbox at odd hours indicate that the other person might be overworked or disorganized. Or, you may decide to interpret this timing as a sign that they are as committed to you as they would be to a close family member. In either case, it's easy to take a handful of data points and come up with a theory.

Therefore, the times you send emails send messages to other people. That's why you should almost never send an email outside of your normal working hours. Don't fire off work messages from your phone while out at dinner or from the parking lot at church. Otherwise, you'll communicate to people that you work at these times, and they can expect progress at these times.

> **Sidebar:** In early 2014, a ruling from a French judge led to a compromise between labor unions and the country's technology business association. The signed agreement states that an employee can choose to ignore their work emails after hours without fear of retribution. To proactively adhere to the plan, several major companies in France have reconfigured IT systems to shut off remote access after 6:00pm.

That doesn't mean you can't jump onto your laptop in the evenings or the weekends to catch up. But instead of actually hitting the "send" button, consider leaving those messages in your drafts folder. Save them to be sent the next time you get into the office. Or, use an email scheduling tool (available as an add-on, and also built into many email systems) to delay delivery until a more appropriate time.

The other element of email timing is the duration between when a message was received and how quickly you reply. When people write messages to ask questions or request action, they are usually ready for the answer immediately. The faster you respond, the more you teach them that you will respond quickly over email. That means if you take longer in the future, they may grow impatient.

A good rule of thumb is to reply to every email no sooner than the following business day. And if you can't abide waiting that long, at least start by waiting until the afternoon for emails received in the morning, or the following morning for emails delivered in the afternoon. In either case, if someone needs you right away, they should call you.

Consider the following conversation between a few colleagues that starts when Lucy comes into Fred's office. Chances are good at least part of this scenario will seem familiar to you:

Lucy: "Hey did you get my email?"

Fred: "I am not sure. When did you send it?"

Lucy: "Oh, about ten minutes ago."

Fred: "Ah. Well I was working, so I wasn't looking at email. Do you need something urgently?"

Lucy: "No, I just had a quick question."

Fred: "Great, well I will certainly be on email before the end of the day, so I'll get to it then."

Lucy: "Oh, ok!"

Establishing boundaries with your time enables you to get out of email and get into the business of getting things done. Choosing when to send and when to reply ensures that you are in control. It puts you back in the driver's seat of your inbox.

The secret to managing the timing of your email is calmness and consistency. Once you change your patterns, don't fall back into your old ways.

And if people start to notice that you seem less responsive on email and start sending follow up messages an hour later, stay the course. Reply to the oldest message. Deal with email on your own terms.

Before you decide to write an email—or reply to one waiting in your inbox—you should determine if email is the appropriate place to have the conversation at hand.

But first, there's one rule that supersedes all others: **if you don't want anyone besides the recipient to read it, don't put it in an email.** In other words, assume everything you write could be published on the front page of a national newspaper.

Other hints that you should avoid writing an email, and instead pick up the phone or have a conversation in person include the following:

- ✓ You are critiquing someone's work or giving negative feedback.

- ✓ You are dealing with anything emotional or sensitive.

- ✓ You are sharing information that is secretive, such as salaries or layoffs.

- ✓ You are brainstorming, discussing ideas, or debating policies.

Once you decide that you *do* want to write an email, the *way* you write it can inspire others. For example, if you always put their name in the message ("Dear Joanna") you may help encourage recipients to think more consciously about email as correspondence.

That way you're writing *to* someone—not just typing *at* someone and issuing commands.

Likewise, keep your emails to just one topic. If you receive an email with multiple topics, consider breaking it up and replying to them individually. If you receive an email where the subject doesn't match the contents, modify the subject line.

You also can influence others with how you use attachments, the *to:* line, the *cc:* line, and the *bcc:* line. Pay attention to the words you employ. Decide what goes in the subject and what goes into the body. Just like in any other form of human communication, it's all about how you say it.

But more on this later: for now, consider the subtle power that your words have over others.

What you write will become what they write.

Making subtle changes to your own actions will begin to influence the behavior of others. You'll teach them how you do things without any direct instruction. You'll inspire transformation without barking orders. You'll make change happen.

But to do this, you need systems. You need patterns that work for you and your colleagues.

You need boundaries and protocols, with scripted interactions and well-defined expectations.

You need a plan. That's why it's time for Part III.

PART III

PATHWAYS AND PATTERNS

Chaos was the law of nature;
Order was the dream of man.

– Henry Adams

Chapter 6

Routing to Systems

When the systems we expect to help us
actually hurt us, we have tragedy.

– Carter Burwell

Now that you know the problem, it's time for the solution.

The answer comes in multiple pieces. The first half is to focus on the systems where you'll direct the information that arrives *from* email. The second is what you *send out via* email.

Behind the inbox there are systems. Ignore them, and you'll be thrashing around forever.

1. Inbound Routing: Organizing What You Get

Email takes time to process, but the majority of time in your life should be spent doing things more important than email. Like a router in a computer network, analyze your messages immediately to determine where they should go next.

Time is the most precious of all resources. That's why your **calendar is the first place to direct much of the information you receive.**

> Here's a key tip to remember: **if it contains a date and time, it needs to go on your schedule or into the trash.** And if what an email describes is going to take more than an hour to do, you should consider putting the work on your schedule.

The instant that you first see the message is crucial. The best time to make a decision about time-bound opportunities—such as events, meetings, parties, deadlines, travel, and so on—is the moment you first hear about them. That's because if you put it off, you run the risk that you'll miss the date, or that your calendar will fill up.

Worse, deadlines and timeframes are often the area where other people are most often unwittingly unreasonable. They set expectations on you without knowing what *else* you have to do.

Critical points for translating inbound email messages to your calendar include:

- ✓ The moment you start to process date and time information is the moment you should decide whether or not to put it on your calendar.

- ✓ If you're unsure if you want to participate, add it your calendar but mark it as "tentative." That way, you have to be intentional about scheduling over the prospective appointment.

- ✓ If you're confident you'll make it, you may want to add two more appointments: one for travel time *to the event* and another for travel time *from the event*.

- ✓ If you're not involved in the appointment but need to be aware when it's happening, add it to your calendar anyway. This is useful for situations like a colleague on vacation, making note of a product launch or campaign, or when your kids are away at camp.

✓ If you know you'll need focused time to complete a task, add it as an "appointment with yourself." This will help keep you accountable, and also let people who can see your calendar know what you're doing.

✓ Add the event to your own calendar *before* you reply to RSVP. If you're interrupted or get distracted during the process, you won't make the mistake of saying you'll be there without actually showing up.

Next up is your task list. The difference between a task and calendar appointment is that the amount of time it takes to complete something on your to-do list should be trivial. It should take only a few minutes.

If it will require longer than that, your to-do item is to investigate the project and schedule time on your calendar to tackle it.

Tasks are intimately associated with email since they so frequently arrive in the inbox courtesy of other people. Sometimes, they are obvious. Other times, these tasks are buried inside convoluted messages. Here's what to do when one shows up:

1. Rewrite the task as an idea. (The information plus the action you must take, and the context, limits, or range of what you must do).

2. Reply to the email and let the other person know you're on it (or that you need to decline or delay), and provide a timeframe if you can.

3. If writing the email triggers you to think of another related task that wasn't part of the request, put that on your list too.

4. Delete the original email.

The order of these steps matters. You want to start by rephrasing the planned action in your own words so that if you're interrupted, you still have the email and have not yet promised a response.

You want to follow up with a message back to the sender so that you can clearly communicate you are on the case. This may seem redundant, but it's especially important when you've set the precedent that you don't reply to email instantly.

You'll also want to wait to see what other possible tasks float into your mind *after* you've accepted the work. After all, you don't want to give yourself more to do without letting the requestor know that you'll be starting.

And finally, you're done with the message that described what the other person wanted. Delete it. If you need it again, your Sent Items folder will contain a copy.

A third fundamental system is your personal address book. Whether you keep a rolodex on your desk, store your contacts in the cloud, or use a small, black notebook, you'll want to process new contact information as soon as you are reading an email.

That way, you won't end up scrambling to find information about a person. Instead, you'll simply look in the right place. Here are some tips to remember:

✓ Just because you've emailed someone for the first time doesn't mean they are your contact. Wait for *them* to send *you* a personal email before adding them to your address book.

✓ Anything someone places in an email is fair game for your records about them. Their email signature will often contain juicy tidbits, such as their cell phone number, mailing address, or favorite quotation. They may mention names of people in their families, birthdates, hometown, past employers, or upcoming travel destinations. If these are things you want to remember, add them to your contacts directory.

✓ Many people say they are "bad with names, but great with faces." Consider saving a picture from their Facebook or LinkedIn profile, so you're more likely to recognize them at the next mixer, conference, or networking event.

✓ People's names change through marriage and divorce, and they sometimes prefer nicknames. Keep notes so you can find people later.

It takes time to add this information up front, but it can be lifesaver in the future. One day you'll be traveling on business and need to send a text message to a vendor. You'll be at a post office needing the mailing address for an overnight delivery. You'll be walking into an interview and realize you spot an old associate—and can quickly confirm the name of their husband and two children. If the information is in your contacts, you'll be glad you saved it.

Plus, you can use it when *writing* email.

Finally, the fourth inbound system is your folders. If you're a solo entrepreneur or you're organizing a household instead of a company department, this is just the directory structure with your computer's Documents section. If you're in a larger enterprise, it might be a shared drive or an Intranet site.

But before you start to deal with an attachment, ponder whether or not a reply is in order *to confirm you received it*. That's because files sent along with an email tend to be highly important and urgent, and people are probably even more nervous about the attachment getting onto the recipient's radar.

And although paper may seem old-fashioned, don't discount the value of a lateral file. It's sometimes easier to deal with well-organized physical archives that you can touch.

Here's a good rule of thumb: if you need to study, edit, or review something in detail, print it out. And if you want to be sure that you have it in hardcopy format to hand to another person or to keep for years, turn those ones and zeros into paper.

But most of the time, you'll want to save any attachments you receive via email to be filed and stored elsewhere. Every document should go to an intermediate storage location first. Consider using the "Downloads" folder established by your operating system. This is already the preferred location for any files you pull off of the Internet. Think of "Downloads" as your *document* inbox. Save anything you receive there, and then go to that spot to decide what to do next with each file.

The second step is to rename the document, since it's almost named something nearly useless like `resume.pdf` or `report.doc`. Consider the following system:

✓ Add a prefix to the filename in the form `YYYY.MM.DD` , inserting the year and month to which the file applies, or at least when you received it. This allows you to sort files by name and scroll to the relevant date, since the operating-system provided "last modified" and "date created fields" don't always line up to what you mean.

✓ Rewrite the filename so it includes the type of document and the topic of the document.

✓ Consider preserving the original filename in parentheses.

For example, if you receive the file `customer surveys` you might change that to be `2015.04.23 X-5200 Series Product Customer Surveys`. That way, you can easily sort by other files in the same folder to locate those produced around the same date, or later replace this one with more recent versions.

Then, place the file in the appropriate location. You'll want to organize your documents into folders and subfolders, or work within your company Intranet. Whatever system you use, think of other people accessing it in the future. You want filenames and file folders that will make sense.

Everything you receive should go into one of four locations: your calendar, your task list, your address book, or your document management system. If there are other places, they should be specific to your job or industry. When receiving anything, get it out of your inbox and into the place where it belongs.

That way, your inbox tends toward empty, and those places where information is supposed to be stored can be made to do their job.

2. Outbound Routing: Organizing What You Give to Others

The computer scientist John Postel is credited with popularizing what has become known as the *robustness principle:* be liberal in what you accept, be conservative in what you send.

This is meant as advice to the designers of computer networks. When receiving data from other locations, assume it may arrived damaged or malformed. But when sending data to a distant system, ensure your own signals are crisp, elegant, and flawless.

Start with your own calendar. It is the vault where you count and protect your own time. Each slot represents a portion of your life. Although Ralph Waldo Emerson could not have imagined the busy 21st century professional when he wrote it, he is still correct with the observation that "the only true gift is a portion of thyself."

Before you send an email, consider the impact on your own schedule. Besides the time to write what appears in the body and to collect whatever you include in the attachments, what part of your future are you promising with this message?

> **Sidebar:** If you're setting up a meeting with someone else, place the time on your calendar *before* hitting the "send" key.
>
> If you can't see their calendar, place tentative times on your *own* calendar first. If you wait until after the email is delivered, you might forget what you suggested. And if you don't actually reserve the time, you may schedule over it before their reply arrives.

Likewise, you may be sending an email which generates more work for yourself. If you're committing to make progress on a specific project, set aside the time on your own calendar before writing the message.

If you're expecting a reply that will require extensive analysis on your part, set aside time for that work before sending the message. Both of these appointments double as a reminder to follow up, either to ask for more time or to check on the status of your own request, respectively.

Most importantly, treat your calendar like a family heirloom. It's tremendously valuable to you, but will be ignored and discarded by almost anybody else. When sending email, make sure you're not promising to give up what you can't afford to offer.

Second, consider your task list. Almost every email that has ever been sent represents a to-do item. When you receive a message, you have work ahead of you—even if that consists mostly of hitting the "delete" button. Likewise, when you're sending an email, you're assigning a task to one or more people.

It might seem like the entire purpose of most messages is to get something *off* of your own task list. But much of the time, sending a request to someone else generates another task for yourself. Work is more like a symphony than it is like a solo. When you hand off the melody to someone else, you need to be prepared to play the bass line, handle the counterpoint, or take back the spotlight later on.

At the very least, when you send an email with a task, make a task for yourself to follow up. None of us are 100% reliable. Messages are deleted, details get lost, plans become muddied. Something might go wrong.

Of course, it's likely that the other person received the message and intended to follow through. Nevertheless, if you sent a task, you still have a task of your own to make sure it got done.

> The effort of following up is not trivial. Your email program likely includes the ability to flag messages for follow up with a star, checkmark, or other icon. Make use of this feature.

Sending off a task to someone else might also trigger thoughts in your mind of future tasks, for yourself or for others. If you ask a colleague to write something, you may need to make a note to review it. If you direct an employee to read an article, you might want to get their feedback.

There's a natural interplay between tasks, and if you don't make a note of the follow-up task for yourself, neither task might get done. Keep on top of what you plan to do.

Next, your personal address book represents a crucial opportunity each time you send an email. When you're writing to someone else, you're telling them something: inviting them to an event, giving an instruction, or providing information, wisdom, or advice. It's hard to remember who you've told what. Your address book is a great place to record this information so that you can strengthen your relationships.

For example, imagine sending a note to a former colleague suggesting they attend an upcoming annual mixer at your company. Consider jotting a note in your personal address book indicating this invitation. That way, you'll be able to review it next year, and decide if you want to reach out again. You'll be able to personalize your message ("I invited you last year and you couldn't make it, so I wanted to be sure to invite you this year!") and show your colleague that you value the relationship.

The personal address book is also a great place to keep track of any technical skills, resources, or relationships that other people have. You'll want to leverage these when sending instructions or special requests.

It's easy to forget which of our contacts has a key connection to an important figure in the industry, or is intimately familiar with a certain software application or has some other area of expertise. Whenever you send a message—especially with someone who you do not correspond with often—consider adding some details to their record in your personal address book.

> **Sidebar:** It might be tempting to use your contacts directory to keep tabs on "who knows what." If you're planning to change jobs, you could record who you've told. If you need to make layoffs soon, you could keep track of everyone who is aware of this plan.
>
> However, tracking these kinds of secrets can become cumbersome and comes with a great deal of risk. Your best bet is to be as transparent as you can with everyone, while at the same time always maintaining the same circles of trust. Use contact records

to keep track of how you can help others and how they can help you, but not what you're mutually keeping under wraps from other people.

Lastly, your folders are an essential outbound system. We usually think of whatever mechanism we use to file away documents as something used for messages that come to us. But the act of sending messages is also an opportunity to review how what we manage is organized in the first place.

Before you attach a document to an email to send to someone else, make sure that document is stored in a reasonable location and has the best possible filename. That way, when you go to find it again, you aren't trying to search through your email's Sent Items. You can go right to the location where it's stored. The desire to send an email with an enclosed file should trigger the desire to ensure that file is kept and labeled correctly.

Perhaps more importantly, though, is deciding if you truly want to send an attachment in the first place. Consider the situation in which you want to relay a piece of company policy to someone else. You could send them the entire 100-page PDF. You might also tell them where to look in that document. But why not pull out an excerpt of the key pages and send that alone? That prevents them from being distracted by all of the content they *don't* need.

Or better yet, copy and paste the text into the body of the email. Or best of all, don't send anything. Instead, tell the other person *where* they can find the policies on the company intranet, so that you don't unintentionally send (and they don't unwittingly save) an outdated version.

Email is a conduit into your brain, but also into your personal organization system. When it's time to write a message to someone else, you are exposing how you manage—or don't manage—your information.

Much of that doesn't need to exist in your own files exclusively. Instead, you can direct people to where it can be found, and devote your time to ensuring that shared resource is available.

Systems are everywhere in our world. Infrastructure often hides just beneath the surface, efficiently shuttling resources and powering our economy.

Your email inbox is a router in the middle of these systems. And for you personally, your calendar, your task list, your address book, and your document folders are the most crucial. These should contain what you need to know for as long as you need to know it—instead of your email inbox.

When information lands in your hands, break it down and place it into the appropriate location.

When ideas enter your mind and are ready to be distributed to others, ensure they are reflected in these systems before you send an email.

Make your own email system part of the solution, not part of the problem.

Work the system for you!

Chapter 7

Routing to People

Our prime purpose in this life is to help others.
And if you can't help them, at least don't hurt them.

– The Dalai Lama

THE MOST IMPORTANT QUESTION about any email—more than the subject, more than the style, more than the attachments—is selecting the people you decide to send it to. Dash off a message to the wrong person and you may be ignored. Or, you may be embarrassed.

A misdirected email can lead to anger, guilt, or grief. Worst of all, you may not realize it and never get the answer you need or successfully kick off the action you requested. So before you even consider writing an email, consider who will receive it.

To ensure that you give the recipient the utmost respect, make sure that the *to:* and *cc:* lines are the last two you complete in the process of writing a message. Not only does this keep people at the forefront of your mind, it also prevents you from accidentally sending a message too soon. After all, you can't send an email to no one. Write the body, then summarize in the subject, and finally add the addressees.

Those are the mechanics around who receives your email. But consider what the person who might receive it will actually do:

Do they have the power or the interest to act upon the idea you want to relay? Not everyone has the capacity to act. They may work in an office where they don't feel comfortable speaking up. They might be overwhelmed with other tasks. They might not have the technical skills to complete your request. And even if they can do what you want them to, they might not be interested in helping out.

Are they open to the information you want to share? New data may supplement old data, but it often challenges assumptions. Change is painful. If you're presenting something in an email that someone didn't know, they may feel foolish. If you're telling them something they already know, they might feel insulted that you think they need to hear it.

In order to do anything useful with your message, the recipient must be open to what you're saying. There's no guarantee your email won't fall upon deaf ears.

Do they trust you? Just because you can send an email to someone doesn't mean they value your advice or consider you to be a reliable source. Email is a great equalizer in access because almost anyone can be sent a message, but it doesn't ensure that people will believe what you have to say.

Trust is not given; it is earned. And just because someone appears to be in the affirmative with their reply doesn't meant they aren't going to do—or say—the complete opposite behind your back.

Is one of you in a position of authority with respect to the other? This is perhaps the most crucial question with regard to the person who receives an email. If they consider you a superior in the company or within the context of the project, they may bend over backwards to get you a response. If they consider you a peer or a competitor, you might not get the answer you want. And if they are your boss, their reply may depend on whether or not they want to support you.

Email interactions often reflect real-world power dynamics, only magnified. That's because it's usually easier to say what you mean in writing, as well as easier to say nothing at all by hitting the "delete" button.

Is this someone who tends to respond to email? Too many people treat their inbox like the scrolling ticker on a 24-hour cable news channel. They feel that the medium is mostly for getting information to them, rather than having some kind of dialogue. And worse, they assume if they don't catch something, it will come around again, eventually.

Is this someone who takes responsibility? Personalities at work are as far ranging as personalities everywhere. Some people like to take on more responsibilities; others are trying to do less and less (even if it's so they can be more effective at what remains). An email is often a task request. Will the person you received it consider this a burden or an opportunity?

Is this someone who appreciates or dislikes reminders? We are all occasionally forgetful. Some people, however, feel a sense of importance when they receive that gentle nudge about a promise they already made. Others get annoyed with the follow up.

Because emails are sent all at once without the chance to read facial expressions or follow vocal cues, it's not easy to know if we're being helpful or frustrating. Figure out what others prefer before moving forward. And if you don't know: try "Please REPLY to confirm you got this message" on the first email to establish a baseline.

Once you begin to consider these questions, you'll start thinking more carefully about who you're sending the email to, and even how you write it. You'll begin to decide if something should even be sent as an electronic message. Perhaps that person would respond best to a phone call or a visit. Or, avoiding the visit might save you time and grief.

Whatever you choose, the people who get your emails are the most important component of any interaction in this corner of cyberspace. The next question, then, is how you decide to address them.

Email is more than a one-to-one communication medium. In fact, there are three distinct channels through which an email can be sent: the *to:* line, the *cc:* line, and the *bcc:* line. Each has its own meaning, and the way you use each one has its own subtext.

Messages must have recipients. This much is obvious. The word "to" implies that this the most direct place to place an email address. If you are only sending a message to a single person, the intention is clear.

But what happens if you want an email to be delivered to two people? What about three? Should the message be sent "to" all of them?

Here's the most straightforward rule to remember: **the more people who receive a message, the less commitment you'll get from each one.** And furthermore, people on the *to:* line are more likely to read your message, take action (and possibly reply) than those merely being carbon-copied. With that in mind, here's a handy reference for many common scenarios:

> **One recipient:** Place them on the *to:* line.
>
> **Two recipients:** If both are equally relevant to the topic message, put them both on the *to:* line. If one is merely being kept in the loop, leave them on the *cc:* line.
>
> **Three to six recipients:** Keep the majority on the *cc:* line if possible. This will discourage long reply-all chains, and reinforce to the crucial people in the *to:* box that they need to do what the message describes.
>
> **Seven or more recipients:** At this point, you may want to consider using blind-carbon copy. This is appropriate as long as you explain that you are doing it in the message, especially if you use the body of the email to indicate who is hiding in the *bcc:* line.

Another way to remember best practices for routing to people is to think of each address line having a different level of significance:

To: These people should be replying to the email (or at least acting on it, if no reply is needed). Therefore, a message should only be sent "to" one person, unless either person could reply.

Carbon-copy: These people need-to-know what's being relayed, but have no direct action. If you're not sure if they must have the information, assume they'd rather not be bothered. We get too much email as it is. Leaving more people off of a routine communication is a welcome relief.

Blind-carbon copy: Avoid using this feature, because no one knows who has been bcc'd. Save it for distributing an information-only message to a large number of people who don't know each other, or for whom a follow-up, reply-all discussion is *not* required. And always indicate *who* was bcc'd, even if it's just a general description of the entire group.

In any case, you may want to seriously consider sending your message multiple times to smaller groups of recipients, rather than to multiple individuals all at once. This takes a little effort, but with skillful copy and paste can be quite efficient.

More importantly it combats the *bystander effect*: the phenomenon where everybody thinks somebody else is going to do something, and nobody ends up doing anything.

To summarize: When a message lands in an inbox that was also sent to two or three or more other people, it's easy to assume that one of those other individuals will take care of it. Unfortunately, when everyone makes the same assumption, nothing actually gets done. **Therefore, you should send to fewer recipients whenever possible.**

No discussion of email is complete without a review of *bcc:* or "blind carbon copy." This feature is so dangerous it's not even turned on by default on many email programs and instead must be explicitly enabled.

People who are bcc'd receive a message in secret, so that no one knows they were included. In fact, if multiple people are on this line, none of them know the others were on that list.

The reason this is a potential landmine is because one of those people might decide to reply-all, exposing themselves to the rest of the group. What was a private conversation is revealed to include one or more secret listeners. Other people feel violated. Email is no longer safe. Trust is lost.

Blind carbon copy also presents the opportunity for profound embarrassment. Consider the following email:

> From: Mary Jones *(employee)*
>
> To: Bob Smith *(boss)*
>
> Bcc: Luke Jones *(employee's spouse)*
>
> Subject: Leaving Early on Friday
>
> Hi Bob,
>
> I just wanted to remind you I'll be heading out at noon on Friday for the weekend. Thanks!
>
> Mary

What happens when Luke casually hits "reply all" to respond to his wife, Mary? He might include a racy detail about their plans for their romantic getaway, which will be forever burned in Bob's memory.

The moral of the story is this: *never use bcc*—unless you tell people you're using it. And the main reason to do that? Prevent others from starting a reply-all chain. After all, nobody enjoys a long discussion over email among dozens of people and countless email messages.

There is one final person involved in every email you write. That's you, the sender.

Although people who receive your messages are likely to at least see them, you're the most likely to *remember* sending each message. The muscle memory of each phrase and word is embedded in your subconscious. While you wrote that email, each recipient's relationship with you—as well as what you wrote and their place within the hierarchy of *to:*, *cc:*, and *bcc:*—will influence their actions. You are the author of your outbound emails, and you must matter if something is going to happen.

With you at the center, it's important to keep messages short and intimate. Others will react if they believe it is part of their responsibility to do so. Focus on the one or two people who need the information. Figure out what they *want* to do, what they *can* do, what they *will* do, and how to include them.

Route to the right people to get the right response. Use the best words and put individuals on the address line that makes the most sense.

Ensure your messages are only sent to individuals who need to be involved.

But when you do, don't just watch your tone and the people you decide to include.

You also need to watch the clock.

Chapter 8

Routing to Timeframe

Time is what we want most, but what we use worst.

– William Penn

ALMOST NOTHING IS TRULY URGENT. Most action steps can wait an hour, or a day, or a week, or even longer. The more important something is, the more it's worth waiting for to get it right.

That's not true of everything, of course. If you need emergency medical treatment, don't put it off until it's convenient for your schedule. If you've got a plane to catch or a tickets to a show, arriving on time is essential.

But email—like the postal mail that inspired its name—is never urgent. If you send an email you should not expect an instant reply. And more importantly, if you receive an email, the worst thing you can do is respond instantly.

Why? Because an immediate reply to a message **trains the other person to believe you will always respond straight away.** You're teaching people to believe that you are there, at the other end of the Internet, waiting to do their bidding.

Emails may be delivered in seconds thanks to the incredible speed of modern technology. But the timing of what you should do with the emails you receive (and what you should expect of others regarding emails you send) is up for discussion.

When you route a message, you're not just routing it to the right system and the best people, but also to a timeframe.

Whether you realize it or not, your email program is a time machine. It controls the rhythm of replies and the distance to important moments in the future.

1. When to process email.

When email first became accessible to the academics at major universities doing research on early computer networks, the only time that one could read or write messages was during brief sessions at the computer terminal. If you were a lowly graduate student, you'd sign up for machine time in the only space available: the wee hours of the morning.

These days, most Americans carry a computer in their purse or pocket that allows them to respond to email from nearly anywhere in the civilized world at any hour of the day or night.

We check email at red lights, we check email when we get home, we check email during dinner, we check email after the kids are asleep, and we check email at three in the morning on the way back from a late night trip to the restroom.

The deeper problem here is the word "check." Email is not like one of a patient's vital signs that must be continuously monitored. Instead, email is *correspondence*. It's not something you "check," it's something you *process*.

The best time to process your email is a function of everything else that is happening in your schedule. Find timeslots in your day in which you can devote at least fifteen minutes to managing your inbox. Close the door to your office, or slip on a pair of headphones. Communicate to others that you are trying to process messages and should not be interrupted.

Of course, this is the opposite of how most people deal with the swarm of messages. They leave their email program open all the time on their computer, always ready to be interrupted by the "ding" of a new message or a pop-up window on the screen.

Instead, turn off these notifications. Minimize the software application that shows your inbox, or better yet, shut down the program completely. Only work on your email during these short windows. The rest of the time, your messages aren't important.

A funny thing happens if you start to ignore your email at the times you haven't reserved for processing. You'll start to find yourself less stressed about the overwhelm of your inbox, and able to be more effective in meetings, conversations, and other areas of work.

And furthermore, other people will start to use email differently when communicating with you. But more on that later.

2. When to send email.

The time that you choose to process your emails doesn't need to be the time that you *send* those emails. In fact, it's often best to have messages delivered at a completely different time. Here's some reasons why:

Communicating Responsiveness: People who send emails pay attention to the amount of time that passes before a reply arrives. Sometimes, messages fly back and forth instantly, like two telegraph operators. Other times, the return email takes days or weeks to appear. Too often, a reply is *never* provided.

Over time, we come to expect responses with a certain time frame because the other person trains us to do so. If you reply straight away, you'll teach people to believe that's what you always do. And of course, nobody can live up to this expectation. Most of us need to be away from our computer or mobile device for meetings, meals, sleep, and actual work. Since no one can see what you're doing when you type out a reply, they imagine you are always available.

Instead, choose how long you will wait before responding. Perhaps you'll respond in no less than four hours, or you'll always wait to the next business day. Select a policy for yourself and be consistent. Within weeks, you'll start to train other people accordingly.

Communicating working hours: Along with a subject line, a body, and various other elements, every email message includes a *delivery time*. That's the exact time and date, down to the second, when the other person hits the "send" button.

This timestamp explains when that person was working. And just like the amount of time that passes teaches people how soon to expect a response, the time the message was delivered indicates the hours that the other person keeps. Messages sent on a weekend, late at night or in the wee hours indicate when you are awake and on the job.

That might seem advantageous at first. Don't we all want to show our devotion by working at late hours?

But in reality, one email sent just after midnight can make us seem like workaholics. This is because people tend to extrapolate on one data point, considering it as representatives. Plus if you're sending messages at 1am, does that mean others should expect a reply at that hour?

Instead, save emails as drafts and send them during working hours. Or use a "delayed delivery" feature of your email program or an add-on. Either way, don't send email when you don't want people to think that you're working.

Expressing the appropriate urgency of email: There are situations in which an immediate reply is needed. These cases often involve tense emotions, furious dialogue, and rapid action. Email is no place for instant communication. If you receive an email which includes an urgent request and quickly hit the "reply" button, you teach others that email should be used for hair-trigger needs.

Instead, resist the urge to fire back. If the problem does require attention at that moment, pick up the phone or walk down the hall. If the only way to effectively respond is via email, add this prefix: "I happened to be checking my email only minutes after you sent this, so I can reply…"

Or better yet, simply wait to reply. If it's really urgent, that phone call will come soon enough.

3. Saving email for later.

Routing your incoming and outgoing messages to a timeframe requires that you have systems for saving items to be processed later. To a small degree this is already handled for you during those precious few hours of sleep when you aren't actively checking your email. But as you change your perspective, you'll need new techniques on how—and where—to squirrel away your messages as well as your intentions.

Storing messages: The worst place that any message can live is in your inbox. That's because we're constantly staring at the pile of emails there in the same way that we become overwhelmed by the piles of paper on our desks. If you're not going to deal with an email when you first see it, you need to store it somewhere else.

Every modern email program gives you the ability to create subfolders, either beneath the inbox or elsewhere within the hierarchy. A great system is a handful of folders that mean anything except for "right now." A good solution, advocated by efficiency expert Merlin Mann, is to create the following:

✓ An "Action" folder for tasks that you need to do but will take more than a minute.

✓ A "Waiting" folder for messages where another person needs to respond.

✓ An "Archive" folder for emails that you've already processed for reference only.

Another effective way to save emails is to set up a folder for each day of the week: one named "Monday," another called "Tuesday," and so on. Whenever you receive a message, drag it to the day that you'll deal with it. Then, make sure that folder is the *first* one you process on the corresponding day.

If you're using an electronic to-do system, you may be able to save emails there by dragging-and-dropping. A similar approach works if you have directories on your computer desktop, or a calendar. As with any filing system, messages are kept out of sight until they need to be processed.

You can also store a message by forwarding it to yourself on a time delay. Your email program may have a feature that supports this, or you can use a tool like Boomerang, FollowUpThen.com, FollowUp.cc, or Right Inbox.

Promising responses: If you receive an email but don't plan to respond within your usual timeframe, you'll cause others to become concerned. An unanswered message is a leading cause of high blood pressure in the workplace.

Instead, do *reply* to the email but don't *respond* to the request. That means you can let people know that you got their note. You've acknowledged they exist.

Your return message can take a couple of different forms: you can make an explicit promise ("I'll get back to you next week.") or you can make a generic claim ("I'm not sure when I'll get to this, but it is on my list.") You can even put the task back on the person asking ("Can you follow up with me after the 15th?")

Of course, a promise must be worded in a way that has a positive effect on the relationship. You should always reply to an email that asks you to do something. But if you reply with "yes, but not yet" be conscientious with what you write.

Planning delivery: The final element of routing to a timeframe is deciding when a message will be delivered. Normally, this is immediately after you hit the "send" button, but just like gathering your wits before making an important phone call, you may want to wait before actually sending your thoughts to the other party.

There are many reasons to plan your delivery time carefully, in addition to communicating your working hours and expressing the appropriate urgency of email as described above. If you know someone will be heading to a meeting at 10:00AM, sending them some final reminders at 9:00AM might be more effective than doing so days or weeks before. Likewise, if you're ahead of schedule on a project, you may want to wait to send in your final deliverable so that it meets the expected timeframe. Otherwise, you might appear to have managed your time poorly.

The easiest way to plan your delivery is to save messages in your Drafts folder. Once the appointed time rolls around, open the email and send it. You can make this your pattern: keep *every* email as a Draft and then send every email at the same time, such as the start of your work day.

You can also create a "To Send" subfolder. But whatever system you use, ensure your messages are actually delivered. There's no point in promising a response if you can't make good on that promise.

Keep in mind that many of the greetings and comments people write in messages reference the time of delivery. If you have a habit of writing "Good afternoon!" or "Have a good weekend!" be conscious of when the message will actually be delivered.

Time is your greatest ally in your efforts to be more productive. There is never enough time today, but there's plenty of room in the future.

If you route messages to timeframes, you build highways that lead to your tomorrows. Instead of feeling constantly pressured, you can start to plan ahead.

Conversations don't have to happen all at once. Instead, they can happen over the course of days, weeks, or even longer.

To win the battle with your inbox, outlast your opponent. Recognize that the people who want instant answers are not being reasonable.

Structure your time and time your replies.

Leverage the reality that time moves ever forward— as well as the reality that most of what we talk about has been discussed before.

To save the most time: find and use ready-made scripts. More on that in Chapter 9.

Chapter 9

Email Scripts for Common Situations

What has been will be again, what has been done
will be done again; there is nothing new under the sun.

– Ecclesiastes 1:9

ONE OF THE MOST FRUSTRATING PARTS OF EMAIL is that it is so repetitive. Messages often feel like echoes of past messages. Typing a response often creates the sensation of déjà vu.

We know that most of the email we write is going to be skimmed at best, and a lot is going to be junked immediately. When you send email to someone else, *how* you choose to write it is going to have a tremendous impact on whether or not it gets read. And if you're going to get a reasonable number of emails written, look for ways to save time.

To write an email effectively, start with a plan. To write an email efficiently, take advantage of work you've already done.

Outline, and then outsource. Define a structure, and then figure out how to produce that structure with the minimal amount of work.

Make sense? Let's take a look at how to make the repetitive process of email significantly less labor-intensive while reducing the amount of brainpower required to process messages.

Consider the following example of a message from a potential customer to a vendor.

From: fred.smythe@corpland.com

To: ldoughy@abagen.org

Subject: hey

Hey, I was thinking about asking you for a proposal for us. I think we could really use your help. We're really struggling with our meetings and maybe you could help out. Also, we have NO budget so keep that in mind. Fred

This may look like a typical email, but it's riddled with issues. The most fundamental problem is with form. **Good messages have a clear and consistent structure.**

You can tell it was unplanned based on the way it was written. The subject line reads "hey." The body is one long rambling paragraph. There's no greeting, no clear questions, no parameters, and no direct instructions.

A great email has the following six essential elements:

1. A specific, detailed **subject line** which summarizes the entire email.

2. A **greeting** which addresses the recipient by name.

3. An **opening sentence** to provide some context for the email.

4. Just one specific question or direct instruction to the recipient.

5. A **closing** sentence.

6. A complete **signature.**

Each of these parts has a definite internal structure, which presents the opportunity to script each one. But instead of covering these standard parts in order, let's look at them in reverse.

Email Signatures: Most people know the meaning of the phrase "email signature." No matter which software application or web-based tool you use for electronic correspondence, there is a feature that lets you attach a block of text to the bottom of every message.

Although we call these "signatures" they might more appropriately be called "letterhead." They contain your name, contact details, and related information about your brand.

Why are signatures so essential to email? Here's a sample message which illustrates the problem:

> Bob,
>
> Sounds great! Just give me a ring when you get to our building and I'll come down. Looking forward to meeting you in person!
>
> -Suzie

That email is a little barren. While it may be friendly and easy to follow, it is clear Suzie and Bob have never met before. And Suzie is telling Bob to give her a call—but has she provided a telephone number?

This problem is easily solved by using a signature. The purpose of this is to provide consistent information which should be included in every email. So what should go in your signature? Here are the bare minimums:

✓ Your first and last name, including your preferred nickname.

✓ At least one phone number where you can be reached.

✓ Your title and the name of the company and the department where you work.

✓ Your physical address.

If you don't have a signature, people can't find you other ways. Be sure to include this information on *every* email. Of course, use the signature feature of your email program to add it in automatically.

Also, here are some bonus items you can include if you like:

✓ Your Skype, AIM, Yahoo, MSN or other instant messenger handle.

✓ Your Twitter or Facebook address.

✓ A link to your LinkedIn profile.

✓ Your company logo or your personal headshot.

Help others to know how to reach you. Make use of your email signature, and never leave people wondering how to contact you in the future.

The Closing: Most sales pros will tell you: a first impression is important, but a last impression makes the difference. People will remember your final handshake and the last thing you said more than almost anything else.

Likewise, you need a final sentence that empowers the other person to act. Often, this can be an expression of gratitude, such as "Thank you!" But usually the best closing is one that restates the purpose of the email.

In fact, you may want to write your closing *first*, because it's what people will read *last*. And the final statement to enter our mind is the one we're most likely to remember.

One Specific Request: Before you can close an email, you need the body of the email. The temptation is to treat this middle section like a buffet line: stuffing everything imaginable into the message.

But that almost never works. People are busy, and they don't have time to deal with multiple points. Instead, put just one point, and write it as succinctly as possible.

If you only cover one item, that one item is the most likely to get done.

Opening Sentence: An email is not a great document like the U.S. Constitution, but it still needs a rolling start. The preamble of the email is the opening sentence. It sets the stage for what you are going to say.

The opener should be a simple sentence like "Thanks for getting back to me" or "I'm glad we're working on this project" or "Welcome to the team."

Think of this as the warm-up to the email. It doesn't need to provide any real information, but it humanizes the interaction. It prepares the reader for what you're about to say. But before that, you need to identify that recipient.

The Greeting: Here's the most often skipped part of an email: the greeting. Whenever you start to write a message to someone else, include their name.

Consider also a friendly word, such as "Hello" or "Hi" up front. If you need something more formal, use

"Dear" and follow their name with a colon instead of a comma.

The Subject Line: Before an email is read and processed, it must be opened. And to get someone else to consider reviewing your message, you need a solid, effective subject line.

Here's the secret recipe for a great subject: qualifiers, action words, and separator characters. Take a look at the following examples:

Bad: Report
Better: Final Report Attached
Best: Amargo Inc: Final Report Attached

Bad: Update on our current project
Better: Status Update, Englewood Project
Best: REPLY NEEDED - Englewood Project Status Update

Bad: Vacation
Better: On Vacation Next Week
Best: On Vacation Wed 5/8 - Fri 5/10

In all of these cases, subject lines that are just one word are difficult to interpret. Adding clarifying words answers the implied *which* question. If it's not totally obvious which particular report, project, vacation, or whatever else you're referring to, make it clear.

Verbs also improve the effectiveness of subject lines. Use an action word to say what you *did* to create the email or to summarize the point of the email. Alternately, you can add a word or two that tells the recipient what to do.

Finally, a separator character like a colon, a dash, or even a comma is a great way to give an email subject laser-sharp focus. These can be used to indicate a general topic and a subtopic, to show a range, or to connect instructions with the topic at hand.

The worst possible subject line? One which is entirely blank. This is so worthless that many modern email programs throw up a warning when you try to do it, and many spam filters catch these emails and toss them aside.

If you want your emails read, write a good subject.

Once you have the basic structure down for a great email, you'll benefit greatly from ready-to-use emails as templates for efficient and effective communication.

This might seem disingenuous. We think of email as a somewhat personal experience, with one person typing at a keyboard with a message intended for another. But just like we have form letters, standard phrases, and even favorite quotations, it makes sense to save time by developing a library of stock material.

Commit these to memory. Or, create and maintain a file on your computer so you can quickly cut-and-paste. Download a text replacement app that lets you program your own shortcuts. Whatever method you use, develop some prepared answers for standard emails and common situations.

Sidebar: If you type the same string of characters over and over again, you'll want to consider text replacement software. These applications run on your computer and wait for you to type a shortcut such as ~wknd, and replace those five characters with the phrase "Thanks for your time and have a great weekend!"

There are dozens of free and inexpensive tools that do this. Search the web for "text replacement software" and find one that works for you. Or, pump up your email signature feature to include more choices. Whatever you do, find a way to spend less time typing.

Before we cover a variety of categories of email templates, consider the all-too-common situation of a message that is a wall of text. When an email arrives that goes on for paragraphs and makes your eyes glaze over, don't reply point by point.

Doing so encourages lots of discussion via the keyboard, which is something pretty much no one wants.

Instead, send the recipient the following email, which the appropriate fields switched out with their information:

Hi {{FIRSTNAME}}

Thanks for the email!

You've clearly been thinking deeply about this.

Given everything you just said, it seems like this is nuanced enough that we need to set a meeting or at least discuss by phone. Please reply with a couple of times you are available for a conversation.

I look forward to our discussion.

Best wishes,

{{YOUR NAME}}

Those long, rambling emails shouldn't be emails. You can't have nuanced discourse with another person by flinging your opinions via the keyboard.

Remember, **email is for routing ideas, not for creating or storing information.**

If someone else is attempting to create a complex dialogue over email, reply with that script and turn the electronic conversation to an actual conversation.

Here's a bunch of other example scripts you can use. Rewrite them to match your own style, but keep them handy.

Great to Bump into You: How often do you go to a conference, come back from a networking event, or randomly encounter a colleague or friend at the grocery store? These things happen so often that you might as well have a ready-to-use template to send after the encounter. Try this:

> Hi {{FIRSTNAME}}
>
> It was great to run into you the other day at {{LOCATION OR EVENT}}.
>
> I'd love for us to follow-up for a one-to-one conversation, if you are available Can you reply to let me know?
>
> Thanks and have a great day!

Now Is Not a Good Time: We all get busy. Sometimes a request will come in via email or telephone to check out a product or just to meet up for coffee, but we are feeling swamped. It's okay to decline this, and here's a friendly way to do so:

> Thanks for reaching out about this!
>
> I would love to get together, but I'm really tied up right now with work and personal commitments. Do you want to touch base again in about {{TIMEFRAME}} to try again? I would really appreciate it.
>
> Thanks for understanding!

Let Me Get Back to You: Sometimes now is not the right time, but you want to let people know that you're on it. Use the following text to explain to others that you will follow up soon (make sure you record in your calendar, your to-do list, or somewhere beside your inbox that you are going to get back to them).

> Thanks for bringing this up.
>
> I can't get to it today, but it's on my radar and I will get back to you by {{SPECIFIC DATE}}.
>
> Thank you for your patience.

That Email Has Too Many Questions: Often, people will fire off a message that rambles on with question after question, with a few updates and asides thrown in as well. These are always problematic because it's easy for the reader to miss something, and the stream-of-consciousness style can often be unclear. Consider this standard response:

> Thank you for this! You covered quite a few points and I want to get them all individually.
>
> Instead of trying to reply in one email, I'm going to respond individually to each topic. That way, we can keep the threads separate (good for my sanity!) and make sure that nothing slips through the cracks.
>
> Okay, replying again in a minute to your first point!

If the above approach seems a bit too pedantic—or if you are corresponding with a colleague that might be little sensitive—there is a more space-efficient version.

When implementing this technique, be sure and maintain the sentences as they wrote it, even if you break them into separate lines. That way, the phrasing will seem familiar.

Also, never fail to quote the original text. If you don't, the other party will need to scroll back and forth to understand what you mean.

Thank you for the questions and the updates. I'm going to respond to each comment from your paragraph in turn:

> {{QUOTED FIRST POINT}}

{{YOUR RESPONSE}}

> {{QUOTED SECOND POINT}}

{{YOUR RESPONSE}}

> {{QUOTED THIRD POINT}}

{{YOUR RESPONSE}}

Stock Phrases, Greetings, and Comments: The templates above cover situations that virtually everyone has seen before. Although most are only a sentence or two, they still take precious seconds to type. Plus, we are all prone to mistakes when keying them in. Here are some examples:

Thanks for your message! I appreciate you following up.

I really enjoyed catching up with you.

Just to make sure we're in contact and I'm not in your spam folder, can you please REPLY to confirm you got this email?

I've attached the latest version to this message. Please discard any older copies you may have.

Thanks for your time and I hope to hear from you soon!

I truly appreciate your advice.

Can I get an answer by the end of the day on Friday? Please reply and let me know if you think that's reasonable.

Are you available to schedule a phone call to discuss? If so, please let me know a couple of times that might work next week.

I will be out of the office next week, so I will get back to you when I return.

I happened to be on email at the same time as you, so I can reply straight away at the moment!

P.S. Would you be interested in receiving our company email newsletter? I'd love to subscribe you (with your permission of course). Please let me know either way.

Of course, you'll want to write your own. You'll need to adjust for your own tone of voice, the culture of your office, and your email partners.

And be careful not to let your stock phrases make you seem generic. Use them, but do so judiciously.

But no matter what, templates save time.

A surprising percentage of our email content is completely predictable. Take a brief stroll down memory lane through your Sent Items folder and you'll notice how often you're typing exactly the same words, often to the same people.

Furthermore, you may notice that complex, nuanced emails are too frequent. Interactions that should have been meetings are happening in long message threads.

Because email is for routing ideas, not for creating or storing information, your messages should be constructed with the highest possible efficiency.

Build messages using a complete, effective structure. Save time using text replacement software, or at least by saving common phrases in a file on your computer.

Remember that there is nothing new under the sun. The emails you write tomorrow are mostly made up of the emails you've written before.

Leverage that fact to save time. Study the past to win the battle for your inbox.

And speaking of the past, it's almost time to review everything we've covered so far.

Chapter 10

What To Do and Not To Do Over Email

Anyone who has never made a mistake
has never tried anything new.

– Albert Einstein

THE WORLD OF EMAIL MANAGEMENT ADVICE is almost entirely dominated by simple suggestions and admonitions. Put simply, there are "dos" and "don'ts" for email. Unfortunately, many are contradictory. Most are stated without support.

Email is for routing ideas, not for creating or storing information. That means there must be best practices for good routing, and bad habits to be avoided.

Category by category, here's what to do and what not to do over email.

1. The process of managing email.

✓ **DO send "thank you" and "got it" messages,** especially to people outside your organization. While these may seem like they waste time, they also reduce blood pressure.

⊘ **DON'T declare email bankruptcy.** If you delete all of your emails and start from scratch, you'll never learn the skills necessary to manage email appropriately.

✓ **DO attach any files before composing your email.** This avoids having to send a second email with "sorry, I forgot the attachment."

⊘ **DON'T file email messages into contextual subfolders,** since no one else can access this data and since the information probably belongs elsewhere. If you need to prove what you did, use your Sent Items as evidence.

✓ **DO engage with every email you receive,** either by replying to it, routing internal details into an appropriate system, and eventually deleting it.

⊘ **DON'T write email when you're angry.** In fact, never send emails that have any emotional content. If people need to hear the tone of your voice, make sure that you are on the phone or in person when you share your thoughts.

✓ **DO use email for coordination.** If you're providing an update, getting the answer to a simple question, or setting up a schedule, sending an email makes sense.

⊘ **DON'T use email for discussion.** This is best done in person or on the phone. If you must have a conversation through a computer network, use a threaded discussion system such as a chatroom or a forum where the entire history is visible to anyone in a logical format.

✓ **DO confirm that your emails are being delivered,** preferably on a live phone call. That way, you and the recipient both know that messages are getting through and implicitly agree they are important. If you can't get someone to even acknowledge they received your email, it's going to be tough to work with them.

⊘ **DON'T deal with the hardest emails first.** When managing a to-do list, always do the most difficult tasks first. But since your inbox is a record of people waiting on you, process as many messages as you can before getting to those which are most stressful. If you need to buy yourself time with those emails, respond and explain that you are working on the item at hand.

✓ **DO consider a separate address for junk subscriptions or email newsletters.** Although modern software applications are better than ever at filtering these messages, and marketing companies are more respectful about unsubscribe messages, a secret to a clean inbox is to keep it focused on individual correspondence. (You can use rules or filters more easily if your bulk email is going to a distinct email address).

⊘ **DON'T worry about keeping your business and personal email separate.** Someone in the IT department may be reading your messages or scanning for key phrases but that's just a reminder not to use email for emotional or sensitive topics.

✓ **DO send more brief emails instead of fewer longer messages.** It may seem like refusing to reply to messages will reduce their frequency, but that will only cause people to follow up. Instead, sending more messages that are far simpler will decrease your overall time spent in email.

⊘ **DON'T use your email as a to-do list.** It's a mailbox full of correspondence from people who are waiting on you, not a bunch of tasks of varying difficulty that you may be doing entirely for your own benefit.

✓ **DO create a new message for a new thread.** Never reply to an old message and start a new topic, because you'll confuse the recipient.

2. The timing of reading and sending email.

✓ **DO respond in a timely fashion.** This means something different for every person and organization, but an email that sits unanswered for weeks is only going to generate frustration.

⊘ **DON'T respond right away.** If you get an email and fire back a response within minutes, you teach people to believe you'll always be available. Delay sending, or at least write "I happened to be on email at the same time as you" in your message.

✓ **DO schedule your email delivery times** so they represent your working hours and your response timeframes. Otherwise, people may interpret that one late night message as your typical working hours.

⊘ **DON'T use an autoresponder all the time.** It's tempting to set up your email program to tell everyone that you aren't checking email all that often, but this is more likely to annoy people than inform them. Save this feature for when you're out of the office for days or weeks at a time—and then only as a last resort.

✓ **DO have a plan for when you won't be answering messages.** Although the automatic response is helpful for people who are trying to reach you when you're on vacation, it's also a security risk—anyone can email you and find out when to rob your home—as well as a recipe for an enormous inbox when you return. A better approach is to have your inbox managed by a colleague or at least your messages forwarded to them.

⊘ **DON'T answer email throughout the day.** Instead, block your time for email, and use the "offline mode" feature. That way you'll be processing messages without being interrupted by new messages.

✓ **DO review your email at the start of the day and the end of the day**. If you don't check email in the morning, you miss any messages that may have come in overnight. If you don't check before heading home, you may be walking into a firestorm the next day. In both cases if an emergency pops up, don't reply. Instead, pick up the phone.

⊘ **DON'T mark emails as unread after reading them.** Deal with the email rather than forcing yourself to read it again later.

✓ **DO leave emails for the next day.** No email message is so urgent that it needs to be processed the day it was received—at least not as an email. If a true emergency is happening, someone will call you, or you need to make a call.

3. Making decisions about recipients.

✓ **DO send email only to the people who absolutely must have the information.** If you're not sure that someone else needs to know, leave them off. We receive too much email to be carbon-copied "just in case."

⊘ **DON'T use blind carbon copy** without saying who was included. You run the risk that one of the invisible people will reply and therefore engender a culture of secrecy.

✓ **DO place both parties in the *to:* line** if they have equal investment in the message and are both expected to act.

⊘ **DON'T type in the recipients to an email message** until you've done everything else. First attach any files, then write the body, and then summarize the body in a subject line. That way you'll never send an email prematurely.

✓ **DO use distribution lists** for general announcements, since these can be automatically filtered by recipients and are already tied to specific interest groups or departments.

⊘ **DON'T add someone to an ongoing thread** with words like "see below." Doing so gives that person a huge task and only further encourages using email for dialogue as opposed to routing ideas.

✓ **DO test a new email address** with a quick, individual message to ensure you've spelled it correctly and worked out the kinks with any spam filters. This will prevent cc-ing them on a message to a large number of people and then having to follow up when it bounces, as well as reducing the chance you'll spread misinformation about their email address.

⊘ **DON'T use reply-all.** It's almost never what you want, and using this feature only encourages others to use it for future discussion. Move the addresses to *bcc:* or move away from email.

4. Determining the contents of email.

✓ **DO keep your emails brief,** usually less than three paragraphs, and avoid making them take longer than one minute to read. The more you write, the more likely it is that people will just skim your email and miss your key points.

🚫 **DON'T skip the courtesy of a greeting with the recipient's name and a sign off**, such as "thank you" or "regards." This humanizes your message and improves the chances they will respond.

✓ **DO ensure your email has a signature**, which includes your phone number and physical mailing address. This is a way that someone else can contact you if your email message doesn't make sense or needs a deeper discussion.

🚫 **DON'T attach files unless you absolutely have to**. Consider providing a link to the latest version of the resource so that people don't hang on to outdated versions.

✓ **DO write a subject line which summarizes the email message**, and write it *after* you've written the body.

🚫 **DON'T use emoticons.** Ever. They are often interpreted as sarcastic, cute, and unprofessional.

✓ **DO reply to confirm receipt of a message**, or that you have accepted or completed a task. Only do this if the person who sent you the email may not be 100% confident you are on the case, such as they work in a different office.

🚫 **DON'T encourage long back-and-forth chains.** Instead, anticipate responses. For example if you are proposing a meeting, email a few options for dates, times, and locations.

✓ **DO explicitly ask people to respond** (at least the first time) but don't use email receipts. This feature of email applications is widely ignored and considered invasive by many.

⊘ **DON'T save gossip, negative opinions, or personnel data in contact records.** If you get this information, delete it from your inbox, and don't save it anywhere that others could access it. Assume your inbox and contract data is public.

✓ **DO save facts, positive and negative**, in people's contact records. For example, save that they speak fluent Japanese, know Adobe Photoshop™, or even the date that their spouse passed away.

⊘ **DON'T make relative references to time** (such as "today" or "tomorrow") because the email may not be opened on the day you sent it. At the very least, write the day of the week, such as "See you tomorrow (Tuesday)."

✓ **DO keep emails to just one topic.** If you want to cover multiple topics, consider sending multiple emails. If you receive an email with a variety of topics, consider multiple replies, or possibly a number list in response.

⊘ **DON'T send someone a calendar request** if you can't see their calendar (or haven't determined the appointment date already). Doing so is presumptuous, because it assumes they are available at that time.

✓ **DO wish people well** in email but don't use email for long, intimate personal messages. If you want to write someone a fond farewell message, consider a handwritten note.

⊘ **DON'T skimp on grammar and spelling** just because it is email. A message is a letter and deserves your full attention. Save the casual style and slang words for in-person and after-hours.

What to do and what not to do is fundamental to developing any new skill. That's why a quick list is so essential to internalize.

Study the dos and don'ts thoroughly. Decide which you can put into practice. Change your process and your philosophy on email.

And once you've got a sense for how you'll work (and how you won't work anymore), take a step back to look over everything you've learned.

Or, turn the page for a full review.

Chapter 11

Winning the Battle

The real man smiles in trouble,
gathers strength from distress,
and grows brave by reflection.

– Thomas Paine

DEVELOPING A STRATEGY FOR DOING BATTLE with your email inbox began in Chapter 1 with a thorough review of the advice that's already out there. And unfortunately, many of those suggestions are pretty terrible.

That's because they make email management into a full-time career: playing librarian for your own correspondence as if it was a sacred archive. Instead, messages are simply momentary bits of text to coordinate real conversations in meetings, or establish parameters for formal documentation developed *outside* of email.

To manage an inbox effectively, consider your email as a system. It should be predictable and resilient. And because email is such a destructive force on everyone's schedules, that system needs to be inflexible. While we can be reasonable, we can't let others walk all over us.

Establishing a system requires a unifying philosophy, and Chapter 2 presented a mantra for email management. **Email is for routing ideas, not for creating or storing information**. The essential question is knowing the meaning of each of those terms, and using email only when appropriate.

Information—such as dates of upcoming events, phone numbers of colleagues, important documents, or other minutiae—doesn't belong in email. Think of your inbox as the core device in a computer network, or as a postal worker deep inside a warehouse. Data is passed along, but never stored. The goal is to get it and get it out of the system as quickly as possible.

That's why Chapter 3 and Chapter 4 emphasize that the first place to begin to better manage your inbox is outside of email entirely. This includes basic concepts in knowledge management: making information actionable, discovering latent categories, selecting a purpose-built system for managing that data, and determining who needs to have the information.

These ideas are muddied by the defaults in your email program. Since the newest messages are the most prominent, we treat emails from yesterday or last week as second-class citizens—even though they represent the people who have been waiting on us the longest.

Likewise, a modern computer or smartphone with lightning fast Internet access means that emails arrive nearly instantly. Instead of the daily routine of checking the mailbox at the curb or in the lobby, we are overwhelmed with new messages minute to minute.

That's why it's so important to change the rules. And as Chapter 5 notes, the big challenge is not modifying your own behaviors, but inspiring others to change theirs.

If you put things into emails that you wish weren't in emails, you perpetuate that behavior. If you respond in ways (or within timeframes) that you don't always plan to uphold, you teach others how to behave. Your patterns not only establish your own parameters for how to route email, but also provide a subtle reminder to the people around you.

Chapter 6, Chapter 7, and Chapter 8 explain routing in detail. First, deciding which of the many non-email systems in your life should receive information from messages or be the source of data that goes into email. Second, which of the people at the other end of the email network should receive your messages—and which you should seek email from.

And finally, the elusive challenge of managing your time with email. Routing isn't just about where the information flows and who it flows among, but when messages are read, processed, and sent.

Learning a new way of thinking is well-served by good examples, and Chapter 9 provides a framework for writing messages as well as scripts for common email situations. Thanks to widely-available software packages, you spit out long, standardized templates with only a few keystrokes.

To wrap up many pages of advice, Chapter 10 includes a multitude of statements in the form of "do this" and "don't do that." Each is a practical interpretation of the mantra: email is for routing ideas, not for creating or storing information. Don't make the mistake of skipping these essential nuggets of wisdom.

That message is the core idea of this book, and the ultimate weapon in taking control of your email inbox. It will not only change your own habits, but influence the people around you.

Write it down. Burn it into your mind. Whisper it out loud.

> Email is for routing ideas, not for creating or storing information.

Once you have that running throughout your brain, you'll have the mindset to tackle messages from a radically new perspective.

Instead of scrambling to reply, you'll be deciding when to respond and doing so intentionally.

Instead of filing thousands of messages into hundreds of folders, you'll be routinely cleaning your inbox and tossing messages into the trash.

And sometimes you'll get down to a state of nirvana: an inbox with zero messages.

So put down the book. Rethink your strategies. Stop composing and saving information in email, and start routing ideas everywhere else.

Process some email, and then close your email program and get back to work.

Email: it's for routing ideas, not creating or storing information.

Your next big idea is waiting.